Success Wisdom

by Deaf and Hard of Hearing People

Created by Karen Putz

The use of "Deaf and Hard of Hearing" in the title is meant to include DeafBlind, DeafDisabled, Late-Deafened, and Deaf Plus individuals. Each page is a reflection of that person's unique perspective.

All submissions in this book are directly
from the participants who have given
their permission to be published.

Edited by Lauren Putz

For bulk orders contact:
karen@karenputz.com

ISBN: 979-8-9891850-5-4

A note from Karen Putz

Shortly after becoming deaf, I transferred from a community college to a university. I was sitting with a career counselor and trying to figure out what I wanted to do with my life.

I wanted to be a newspaper reporter or a labor and delivery nurse. I was leaning more toward becoming a nurse, because I struggled in my journalism class as a hard of hearing student in high school.

The career counselor listened to my story of growing up hard of hearing and suddenly becoming deaf. We discussed the nursing career track. The obstacles seemed insurmountable.

How would I use a stethoscope?

How would I hear the doctor's orders?

What if I misunderstood the name of a medicine and gave the wrong one?

How would I get around using the phone?

How would I understand a patient?

At the end of the hour, I was feeling quite dejected. I ended up picking a counseling career track.

Years later, I met a hard of hearing nurse who worked in the surgical unit.

Then I met a deaf doctor.

A deaf vet.

A deaf nurse who worked in the emergency room.

A deaf dentist.

A deafblind firefighter.

Deaf and hard of hearing lawyers, scientists, musicians, engineers, pilots, the list went on and on.

You'll meet some awesome people in this book.

This is a book I wish I had way back in the early days of my journey.

Success Wisdom is really not about the usual things that we associate with success – it's really about the wisdom in our hearts and how we can make our mark on the world.

Ultimately, success is however you define it. Success is personal.

It's my hope that you'll take the wisdom that is shared here and create your own path of success that's right for YOU.

Love,
Karen Putz
karen@karenputz.com

"Schools are full of plenty of formulas, but the one I believe every person should learn is: Courage + Dreams = Success. Have the courage to dream big and if you do, success will be within your reach."

Marlee Matlin
Actor and Author

Marlee Matlin is the first deaf and youngest person to win an Academy Award for Best Actress. Her foray into acting began when she played the role of Dorothy in the **Wizard of Oz** at seven years old. Marlee has starred in **Seinfeld, The West Wing, Law and Order SVU, The L Word, Switched at Birth, Glee, What the Bleep Do We Know!?**, and **Quantico**.

Her recent movie, **CODA**, won an Oscar for Best Picture. Marlee made her Broadway debut in **Spring Awakening** and she is also the author of several books.

www.marleematlin.com

> "First, master your skills to claim your space; then, excel to shatter stereotypes. Your ultimate goal: create impact, not just impressions."

Alex Jones
Financial and Real Estate Coach

Alex Jones is a Deaf and Black entrepreneur and a certified coach dedicated to empowering individuals to reach their full human potential. As the founder of ASLCoach Strategy Partners, he specializes in coaching services that span financial, entrepreneurship, and real estate coaching.

Alex holds a Bachelor of Science in Business Management from Gallaudet University and a Master of Science in Human Resource Development from the Rochester Institute of Technology. A commitment to evidence-based practices and lifelong learning underscores his multi-disciplinary approach.

www.alexjonescoaching.com

> "Lay out your life goals and aim to reach them. Your goals are like climbing the mountain; it won't be easy with all the obstacles in the way, but when you get to the top, it's the biggest reward."

Adrean Mangiardi

Filmmaker

Veteran Filmmaker of over 20 years in the video media industry, with a focus on accessibility. Jack of all trades in all stages of production. Reliable, dependable, and determined to see projects through to their deadlines. Known for out-of-the-box ideas, creative solutions, and quick critical logistic planning. Committed to evolving film techniques and adaptable video editing. Enthusiastic about collaboration and group output.

www.mangiardifilms.com

"Always remember that no matter how poor, popular, or successful you are, you will never be superior or inferior to anyone. Knowing and preserving your self-worth is the key to unlocking your successful life.

Whenever a big or small opportunity to shine is presented to you, dance as if everyone is watching!

As you cruise through the path of life, you will face many challenges; what matters most is that you continue to stay persistent, resilient, and practice self-preservation. The more obstacles you overcome, the more self-aware, stronger, and wiser you will become. Success begins when you start to get comfortable with who you are."

Isidore V. Niyongabo

Isidore V. Niyongabo

HR Professional and International Inspirational Speaker

Isidore Niyongabo, MA, SHRM-SCP, is a distinguished global Human Resources leader and the President Emeritus of the National Black Deaf Advocates (NBDA), having served two terms from 2019 to 2023. As the founding Executive Director of International Deaf Education, Advocacy, and Leadership (IDEAL), Inc., Isidore has dedicated over two decades to advocacy, beginning in Burundi and Uganda and extending to the United States. He played a pivotal role in advancing American Sign Language education equity at San Diego State University and in various workplaces. Isidore also represented NBDA on the Federal Communication Commission's Disability Advisory Committee for eight years, focusing on enhancing communication access for individuals with disabilities.

Originally from Burundi, Isidore's life took a transformative turn after surviving spinal meningitis and becoming Deaf. Despite facing early educational challenges, he moved to California, where he earned a Bachelor's degree in Psychology from San Diego State University and a Master's degree in Peace and Justice Studies from the University of San Diego. As one of the few Deaf Americans certified as a Senior Human Resources Professional by SHRM, he emphasizes advocacy, engagement, accessibility, equity, inclusion, and belonging in all his endeavors. Outside of his professional work, Isidore enjoys spending time with his Burundian-Portuguese-American CODA daughter and continues to promote Deaf education and quality of life through IDEAL, traveling globally to share his inspiring story and advocate for a more equitable, diverse, and inclusive world.

5

Melody and Russ Stein

Melody: Melody Stein, born into a family of entrepreneurs in Hong Kong, is a third-generation business owner. She earned a Bachelor's degree in Hospitality Management from San Francisco State University before fulfilling her childhood dream of entrepreneurship. Since 2007, Melody and her husband, Russell, have founded several ventures, including a restaurant and a business education and consulting service. In 2021, she launched MxT 2510, a sustainable clothing brand, with her daughter, Taysia Stein. Her latest venture, Pi00a, was launched in August 2023 with her family.

Russ: After earning his Bachelor's degree in Business Administration at Gallaudet University, Russell began his career by working in relay services at Relay America and then Communication Service for the Deaf, where he launched the first video relay service nationwide with three people. Russell co-founded six businesses with his wife, Melody, including Mozzeria, a Deaf owned-and-operated Neapolitan pizzeria in San Francisco. He also co-founded an international consulting business, Yantern, for Deaf small businesses and future entrepreneurs while operating a ghost kitchen, Pi00a, that focuses on frozen Neapolitan pizza distribution and catering private events. As the Director of the Gallaudet Innovation and Entrepreneurship Institute, Russell oversees innovative strategic planning, several events including the Bison Tank Competition, ten Fellows, collaborations with the Small Business Administration, and other entrepreneurship projects with fellow and future entrepreneurs.

"Live life with passion by pursuing what truly excites you and gives you a sense of purpose. Success follows when you dedicate yourself fully to your goals, putting in consistent effort and hard work. Embrace challenges, learn from failures, and celebrate small victories along the way. Remember, passion fuels perseverance, and perseverance drives success."

Melody and Russ Stein
Entrepreneurs

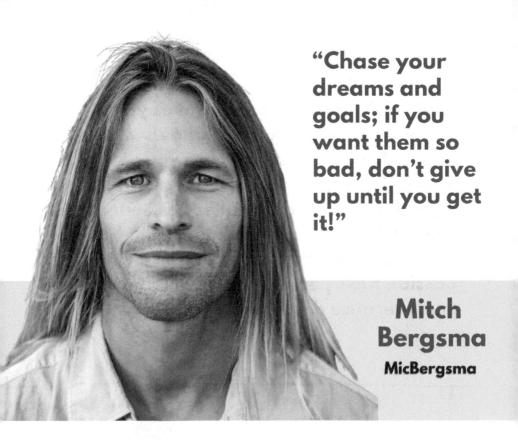

"Chase your dreams and goals; if you want them so bad, don't give up until you get it!"

Mitch Bergsma
MicBergsma

Born and raised on a dairy farm, I played ice hockey and was the only deaf kid in a family of five. I have a passion for wakeboarding and warm weather. At 20, I escaped Washington State on my own, living in Colorado and Florida for a year each before settling in Texas. I competed extensively in wakeboarding, started YouTube channels focusing on GoPro tips and scooter how-to videos, and met my wife Lori, marrying her in Hawaii.

I then delved deep into a 1967 VW bus restoration series on YouTube. Seeking the next chapter, we moved to Hawaii, where I now live the life of a YouTuber, scooter mechanic, in-line hockey player, and VW bus owner.

www.youtube.com/MicBergsma

> "Meet yourself where you're at – give yourself grace and step into the beautiful experience that is being human! Life is presenting everything that you could ever need or want – that hardest part is getting out of your own way to receive it."

Dr. Michelle Hu
Pediatric Audiologist

Michelle Hu has been a pediatric audiologist for over 15 years, working specifically with identification, hearing amplification, cochlear implant evaluation, and aural rehabilitation. Her mission is to empower parents of DHH children and DHH individuals to feel confident in making choices best fit for them and their family dynamics.

Something unique about Michelle is that she grew up hard of hearing herself. She was fitted with hearing aids at three years old and now utilizes bilateral cochlear implants. She is the creator of Mama Hu Hears, a safe space to share, laugh, learn, and inspire others about living life powerfully while being deaf or hard of hearing.

www.mamahuhears.com

Alicia Wooten

**Immunologist and
Co-Founder of Atomic Hands**

Dr. Alicia K. Wooten (she/her) is a trailblazing deaf immunologist and associate professor of Biology at Gallaudet University. Alicia grew up in south Texas as a first generation Japanese-American discovering her deaf identity and love for science over the years. She learned ASL starting in high school and went on to the Rochester Institute of Technology (RIT) to get a degree in Biomedical Sciences. With her love of the medical side of biology, she completed a Ph.D in Molecular and Translational Medicine from Boston University. Her research spans lung biology, infectious diseases, and the immune system. Alicia has explored HIV, autoimmune diseases, and pneumonia-causing bacteria.

Throughout her years in school, she noticed the lack of resources and network for deaf people in STEM. Her desire to change this led to the founding of Atomic Hands, a non-profit that promotes STEM engagement through American Sign Language (ASL). Atomic Hands was created with the ideas of Alicia and Dr. Barbara Spiecker, her other science half. Alicia is dedicated to making science accessible to the deaf community and other minority groups. Passionate about inclusive science communication, Alicia advocates for more diversity in STEM fields and hopes to see more deaf youth exploring their love for all things STEM.

www.atomichands.com

Alicia Wooten

"There are so many ways to live life! I knew early on I wanted to show the world what I could do. Growing up with people underestimating me, I had the mindset of 'watch me prove you wrong.' That gave me a lot of fire to try different things and to keep getting back up when I failed. Most people don't like to admit failure, but for me, failing and figuring out how to try again is how I made it through. Thinking like a scientist, you have to find different ways to achieve your goals and this lets you become more creative, a thinker, a problem-solver, and more motivated for the next thing you can accomplish.

It is also important to learn how to get past that thinking stage where you have ideas, but you're not sure where to start. Sometimes you just have to pick one idea and run with it. For years I have struggled with having ideas and doing nothing about it, but one day I just got up and did it. Because of this, a nonprofit was created, I have a Ph.D and I'm teaching students, I'm learning how to become a better woodworker, I became a scuba diver, and I'm having fun with life."

Melinni "Mel" Taylor
"That Deaf SS lady"

I am a certified Community Work Incentives Coordinator based in Austin. Deaf and fluent in ASL, I hold Bachelor's and Master's degrees in Social Work from Gallaudet University. Previously, I worked as a case manager and as an addiction counselor for non-profit agencies. I work with individuals and organizations to advise them on issues, procedures, and matters related to the Social Security benefits program.

I understand the role that we play in our clients' lives. The work can be difficult, but it is important and fulfilling.

As one of the few Certified Community Work Incentives Coordinators fluent in ASL, I am able to connect with my clients in a way that truly helps them understand and manage their Social Security Benefits. For most people who receive SSI/SSDI, these benefits are a crucial lifeline and the primary means of supporting themselves and their families. Unfortunately, confusion and disruption of benefits occur far too frequently and come with serious and negative consequences.

www.deaffutureworks.com

Melinni Taylor

"Being true to yourself is really the key. You are special. There is no one else in this world quite like you. Your unique combination of skills, talents, and experiences make you truly one-of-a-kind. Embrace this uniqueness and allow it to guide you on your journey. Discover your passions and pursue them wholeheartedly.

Find something that excites you, something that ignites a fire within your soul. Whether it's a hobby, a career, or a cause you believe in, give it everything you've got. When you are passionate about what you do, success naturally follows.

Avoid the trap of comparison. It's easy to look at others and feel inadequate or envious of their achievements. But remember, their journey is different from yours. Focus on your own progress and celebrate your accomplishments no matter how big or small. Each step forward is a testament to your dedication and hard work.

Lastly, remember that happiness and contentment come from within. Seek joy in the simple things (like a good cup of coffee), practice gratitude (like the beauty of nature), and surround yourself with positive influences. Take care of your physical and mental well-being, as they are the foundation for a fulfilling life. I believe in you. I believe that you have the power to create a life filled with passion and success. Trust yourself, follow your heart, and never stop believing in the incredible person that you are!"

"Being versatile allows us to embrace limitless possibilities in life. While we may not have control over our birth, we have the power to shape the way we live it. Passion acts as a fuel, igniting our potential, inspiring us to venture into uncharted territories, and guiding us towards a life filled with purpose and fulfillment."

Gideon Samara
Mr. Versatility

I'm a passionate cook with a love for wine and a keen eye for street photography. Fashion and adventure fuel my fearless spirit.

I am a Sponsorships, Exhibits, and IP Manager for the Office of External Affairs at the National Technical Institute for the Deaf.

> "Find the courage to dive into your passions as if the ocean has no bottom, and you'll discover depths you never knew existed. Nurture that passion well as it is what sets your soul on fire, for it shall light your way through the darkest and coldest part of that very ocean. Remember that success is not a destination – it is a journey of small victories and valuable lessons learned along the way."

Ryan Maliszewski
Changemaker

Ryan Maliszewski is a high-energy strategist, entrepreneur, investor, executive-level consultant, and motivational speaker. Ryan is the Founder and "Chief Hacking Officer" of SiloHack.

Prior to SiloHack, Ryan was the Chief Executive Officer of Mozzeria, a Deaf-led pizzeria. Ryan was previously the Executive Director of the Innovation and Entrepreneurship Institute at Gallaudet University. Ryan also served as an Executive Strategy & Technology Advisor for the Federal Bureau of Investigation (FBI), worked for Booz Allen Hamilton as a senior consultant for various government clients, and on Capitol Hill, worked for both the United States Senate and House of Representatives after graduating from the University of Arizona in Business Management.

Ryan presented at TEDx University of Maryland to talk about "DeafGain," highlighting how Deaf people navigate through life constantly adapting, problem solving, and bringing innovation to the table.

www.silohack.com

Natasha Ofili
Actress, Writer, Filmmaker

"You have to stay true to yourself. By staying true to yourself, you will embark on the path of success. For me, as Natasha, me, being who I am, I am very open, connected, and passionate about what I am doing and what I am trying to achieve, all while enjoying the process. Of course there are challenges that you will encounter every step of the way. You will feel like you want to give up. What doesn't let me give up is the passion inside me. That passion always reminds me why I do what I do, how I continue to be successful, and why I use my platform to make an impact in any way possible."

Natasha Ofili

Being an artist, writer, and storyteller started at a young age, but Natasha did not realize this passion would bloom later in her life. Growing up being the only deaf child in her family meant being solitary in her world of imagination and observation. Natasha loved going to the library and reading stories to ignite her imagination. Stories and music are a way for Natasha to tap into her inner emotions and accept how she sees the world. She loves and believes in the power of storytelling that invokes feelings of human connection, openness, and learning, driving her passion for acting, writing, and filmmaking.

As a rising actress, Natasha Ofili was recognized for her breakout role as Principal Karen Vaughn in Ryan Murphy's Netflix series, **The Politician**, with Oprah Daily singling her out as "a host of newcomers that manage to steal the screen" from the show's seasoned actors. Ofili achieved historical milestones by winning the 2024 Game Accessibility Conference award for Best Representation for her portrayal of Hailey Cooper, the first Black Deaf playable character in Marvel's **Spider-Man 2** video game. She also played Hailey in the Marvel's **Spider-Man: Miles Morales** video game. In collaboration with Coldplay, Pulse Films, and Director Ben Mor, Ofili developed the story and creative direction for the music video for **feelslikeimfallinginlove**, Coldplay's first single on their new album, **Moon Music**, as the Creative Director and lead performer.

Her other credits include Amazon Originals' animated series **Undone**, where she is the first Black Deaf animated character. A Writers Guild of America West (WGA) member, she was a staff writer on the Starz/Warner Brothers' **Untitled Show**, produced by Ava DuVernay's production company, ARRAY. Founder of NIOVISION Productions, she wrote, acted, produced, and directed her award-winning short film, **The Multi**, which was accepted by 14 film festivals, with several being BAFTA, Oscars, and Canadian Screen qualifiers. In the theater world, she wrote her first play, **The Window**, workshopped by NIOVISION, WACO Theatre (founded by Tina Knowles and Richard Lawson), and Deaf West Theatre.

www.natashaofili.com

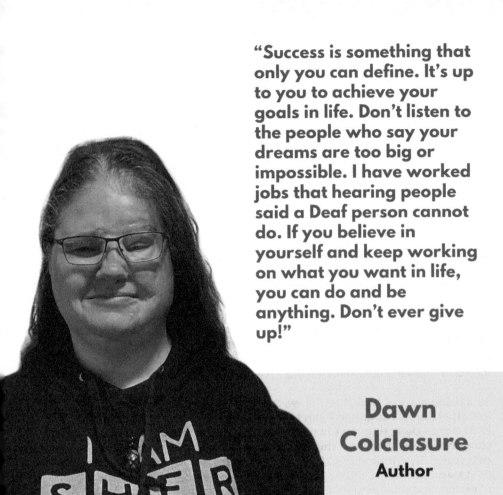

"Success is something that only you can define. It's up to you to achieve your goals in life. Don't listen to the people who say your dreams are too big or impossible. I have worked jobs that hearing people said a Deaf person cannot do. If you believe in yourself and keep working on what you want in life, you can do and be anything. Don't ever give up!"

Dawn Colclasure
Author

Dawn Colclasure is a writer who lives with her husband and children in Oregon. Her articles, essays, poems, and short stories have appeared in several newspapers, anthologies, magazines and E-zines.

She is the author and co-author of over five dozen books, among them **BURNING THE MIDNIGHT OIL: How We Survive as Writing Parents**; **365 TIPS FOR WRITERS: Inspiration, Writing Prompts and Beat The Block Tips to Turbo-Charge Your Creativity**; **Love is Like a Rainbow: Poems of Love and Devotion**; **Parenting Pauses: Life as a Deaf Parent**; **On the Wings of Pink Angels: Triumph, Struggle and Courage Against Breast Cancer**; **A Ghost on Every Corner**; **The Yellow Rose**; and her latest novel, **Imprint**.

www.dawnsbooks.com and www.dmcwriter.com

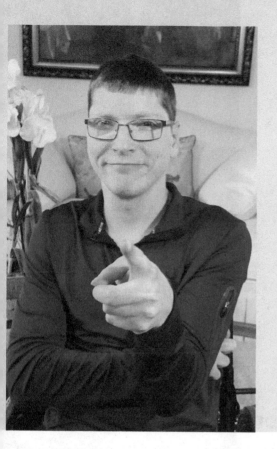

"Live Your Best Deaf Plus Life. Keep Moving, Stay Strong, and Stay Positive."

Jeremy Smith
Deaf Plus Advocate

Jeremy Smith has lived with many challenges related to disability, including his profound hearing loss and use of a wheelchair. He has fully participated in community engagement and there are many examples of his lifelong aspirations to be a role model and supportive advocate for himself and others with disabilities. Jeremy was raised in Northern Virginia and is from a loving family of parents and a brother, who have all learned sign language to communicate with Jeremy. His mother shared that his early years were fraught with numerous medical issues from an early age including Mitochondrial Metabolic Disease, ataxia, deafness, and ADHD. Mobility problems worsened, resulting in Jeremy using a wheelchair from his high school days to the present.

Jeremy serves on the Board of Directors at the Northern Virginia Resource Center for Deaf and Hard of Hearing Persons and volunteers at the Endependence Center of Northern Virginia. Jeremy runs the Deaf Plus Advocate social media channels, which cover his experiences having more than one disability (and many abilities!). He uses humor and creativity as he shares information about his life and access to all activities of daily living.

www.deafplusadvocate.com

"Passion fuels success. Find what you love, invest in your knowledge, and share it with others. Success isn't just about growing wealth; it's about empowering those around you to achieve financial independence. Stay committed to learning and helping others, and you'll build a legacy that goes beyond financial gains."

Dina Rae Padden
The Finance Maven

Dina Rae Padden is the visionary founder of Gather and Trade, a finance service and education company dedicated to empowering individuals through financial literacy, taking control of their finances, and growing money. With a rich background as a former school principal, Dina spearheaded an innovative finance literacy program for high school seniors.

Before her entrepreneurial journey, Dina honed her expertise as a financial analyst and auditor at one of the Big Five accounting firms. Her robust experience in finance, combined with her status as a CPA candidate, equips her with a deep understanding of financial systems and regulations.

Dina is also a financial consultant, bookkeeper and tax preparer, committed to helping individuals and businesses manage their finances effectively. As an entrepreneur, she is passionate about growing wealth and sharing her extensive knowledge with the Deaf community, ensuring that financial empowerment is accessible to all.

www.gatherandtrade.com

"Knowledge and advocacy are powerful forces. If you don't tell people what you need for communication access, others will make the decision for you!"

Dr. Tina Childress
Techy Tina and Communication Access Engineer

Dr. Tina Childress is an audiologist and advocate, drawing from her unique perspective as a late-deafened adult with cochlear implants. Her dedication lies in promoting accessibility for individuals who are Deaf/Hard of Hearing/DeafBlind/DeafDisabled through education, collaboration, and advocacy. During the day, Dr. Childress works as a pediatric audiologist and trainer in various school settings.

Dr. Childress is a mentor to adults and children, subject matter expert, technical consultant, adjunct lecturer, active Executive Board/Committee member and professional speaker. Dr. Childress is a content creator at See.Hear.Communication.Matters. She is renowned for her expertise on topics such as Hearing Assistive and Access Technologies, apps and captioning options in virtual and in-person settings.

Also known as Techy Tina, and as a Communication Access Engineer, she looks at situations where there is a communication breakdown and comes up with solutions that involve low-tech and high-tech tools. She is a go-to resource when people need practical information on how to make this happen.

www.TinaChildressAuD.com

"My advice for you is to follow your heart and do what makes you happy. You will find your path, and even if you fail, keep trying until you succeed."

Kasmira Patel
Founder, CEO of Girl and Creativity,

I was born in India, and my parents found out that I'm deaf when I was a kid. They left India and moved to the USA when I was seven years old to give me a better life and a Deaf education. They enrolled me in New York School for the Deaf in White Plains. I then went to RIT (Rochester Institute of Technology), where I earned a Master's degree in Human-Computer Interaction. After graduating, I worked at Johnson & Johnson as a UX Designer in NYC.

During the COVID-19 pandemic, I was laid off. I felt depressed and lost, unsure of what to do with my life. It was a dark time, and finding a new job was especially difficult.

One day, I had a realization: I wanted to start my own small business, Girl and Creativity. This business is about empowering people to love their bodies through apparel featuring ASL designs. Girl and Creativity has become an amazing platform for Deaf culture, helping people learn American Sign Language (ASL).. Our mission is to make everyone feel welcome and empowered through ASL, teaching and showcasing the beauty of ASL and Deaf culture.

Entrepreneurship runs in my family; my parents were entrepreneurs who owned stores in New York. I believe I inherited this entrepreneurial spirit, which drives me to run my own business. Additionally, my husband and I have taken on a Dairy Queen franchise in Cincinnati, Ohio, where my husband handles the Dairy Queen while I run Girl and Creativity.   www.girlandcreativity.com

"I highly encourage you to find your true passion and keep exploring what you want, without fearing any mistakes or regrets. You have to motivate yourself to make your dreams come true. Don't wait."

Isabel Lainez

Artist, Illustrator, Designer

My name is Isabel Lainez. I was born in El Salvador and moved to Canada when I was 10 years old. Currently, I am a resident of the US. I graduated in Graphic Design from the Rochester Institute of Technology in New York. Afterward, I set up my small business called Izalaix Design. I've been an artist my entire life, ever since I was born. I am thankful to have my grandpa, who saved my artwork for years. He knew I would be an artist one day, and it came true. I am self-taught and continuously explore to find my passion. I never stop pursuing my dreams, which is why I am where I am now.

I have a second small business called Girl and Creativity, where I am the Creative Designer and Owner. Started in 2020, it's a business that spreads self-love to communities, empowering and inspiring them through our products and apparel.

www.izalaixdesign.com

"Be bold. Have the courage to fail often, to be comfortable in the uncomfortable. The path ahead is never straightforward, but becomes easier when you build with empathy and forge strong partnerships."

Toby Fitch
Product Designer

Toby Fitch is a Deaf Senior Product Designer at Microsoft who dabbles in all things creative. He is a passionate advocate for co-design, bringing inclusivity and equity to the forefront of product making.

A graduate of Rochester Institute of Technology's New Media Design program, Toby is committed to transforming the field of design to include historically underrepresented and disabled artists.

www.tobyfitch.com

"Every day is a new page. Enjoy life! Life is not a rehearsal."

Liz Tannebaum
Actress

Liz Tannebaum, an Actress and Executive Producer, is a veteran in the film industry and in the theatre world. As a young child, she got her start acting at age nine and then got started by watching and learning from her late father, Ted Tannebaum, of the renowned Lakeshore Entertainment. Liz is following her father's footsteps by supporting the Deaf arts, theatre, and film. The feature film, **No Ordinary Hero**, the SuperDeafy Movie, was acquired by Netflix and Liz invested and became an owner of this film as an Executive Producer.

She has an extensive background not only in film, but also in theatre. Liz is well-known for her appearance as Sarah in the theatrical production of **Children of Lesser God** and for **WHAT WOMEN WANT**, a film produced by Paramount Pictures. For the stage show, **Staring Back**, as an actress, Liz and fellow cast members were recognized with a CHICAGO EMMY AWARD. Liz's last film was **WHAT?** with John Maucere in Los Angeles. And not only acting, Liz got her feet wet in the world of comedy, first appearing in a one-woman show from the AMERICAN COMEDY INSTITUTE in New York City at Caroline's Off Broadway.

Rosa Lee Timm
Innovative Artist

Rosa Lee is a prominent deaf performance artist widely recognized for her American Sign Language music videos and her lead role in ASL FILMS' feature film, **Versa Effect**. Additionally, she successfully ran her one-woman show for a 20-year period, showcasing her dedication to the craft.

With a diverse background spanning over two decades, Rosa Lee has cultivated her skills in marketing, entrepreneurship, and entertainment. Currently, Rosa Lee holds the position of Division President at CSD Social Venture Fund, where she contributes her expertise to the venture capital and marketing industries as one of the few BIPOC Deaf women in leadership roles.

Rosa Lee's academic journey includes obtaining a bachelor's degree in Social Work from the Rochester Institute of Technology. She further pursued her passion for helping others by earning a Master's degree in Vocational Rehabilitation Counseling from Western Oregon University.

Rosa Lee's commitment to community advocacy, combined with her artistic talents and business acumen, has positioned her as an influential figure in the realm of performance art. Currently, she resides in Maryland along with her two young children and partner.

www.rosaleetimm.com

Rosa Lee Timm

"Finding your passion doesn't follow a set timeline. It's okay if you're unsure where your passion truly lies or if it evolves over time. The key is to let go of trying to control the outcome and allow it to come to you naturally. You might feel that your time isn't well-spent or that your efforts aren't leading anywhere, but you'll be surprised how all the small steps you take become part of the journey. These steps are the building blocks leading you to a place where everything falls into place. You'll realize that all the things you've learned along the way have led you to where you're happiest. To me, that's a success."

"Never be afraid to get back on the horse, especially if it's not the one you fell off. The most valuable legacy my parents gave me was never to fear failure, but to keep on trying until I found something I was good at. Those violin and trumpet lessons may have been painful for my teachers, but they showed me that producing music simply was not for me. Eventually I learned that the typewriter was my instrument."

Henry Kisor
Author

Henry Kisor is a retired journalist, private pilot, and author of ten books, including **What's That Pig Outdoors?: A Memoir of Deafness.** Henry worked as a book editor and literary reviewer for the Chicago Sun Times.

He lives with his wife Deborah and service dog Trooper in a retirement community in Evanston, Illinois.

www.henrykisor.com

> "Keep working hard every day and amazing things will come to you."

Dalia Ottallah
Deaf Plus Advocate

My name is Dalia Ottallah and I am 18 years old. I love to hang out with my family and friends and watch foreign TV shows. In the fall, I will be attending RIT and will be majoring in Cybersecurity.

I was born in Louisiana about 10 miles outside of New Orleans. I love crawfish and watching the Mardi Gras parades marching down my neighborhood.

I was born with severe to profound hearing loss and I have been using a cochlear implant since I was one year old. I mainly use listening and spoken language, but am learning more ASL every day.

"When I was in my early twenties, I had no idea what I wanted to do with my life. I came across an activity where I had to design my 'perfect 24 hours'. I was still befuddled. So I started with the opposite: What kind of 24 hours did I absolutely NOT want? That was easier. After that, I was able to open my mind and imagine a truly incredible lifestyle. Thinking that it was merely fantasy, I allowed myself to go wild. Over a decade later, I found myself living what felt like a perfect 24 hours several times. It took dozens of vision boards, roadmaps, planners, and ongoing conversations with myself to get to a place that once seemed like a fantasy but now feels very real. It all starts with your imagination. No matter where you are in life, you are never stuck. Life is truly within your grasp, you just gotta get in the driver's seat and steer.

Leila Hanaumi
Creator, Performer, Writer

Leila is a Deaf Asian creator, performer, writer, Mompreneur, and accessibility advocate. Her recent ASL performance for **Barbie** earned her critical acclaim and she had the opportunity of a lifetime to interview Margot Robbie onstage after the film's community screening. Using her platform to spread awareness about Deaf culture, she was invited to present during Microsoft's Ability Summit. She enjoys getting involved with theatrical productions as an actor and director of artistic sign language. As a creative outlet, she produces and performs ASL song covers, which have totaled over a few million views online.

Under her lifestyle brand "Today I Awaken," she creates and sells planners. Her planner helps her juggle different roles and make time to enjoy the little things in life with her husband and children. Oh, and twice a year she makes custom cakes from scratch for her children's birthdays!

www.todayiawaken.com

30

"When I was in my early twenties, I had no idea what I wanted to do with my life. I came across an activity where I had to design my 'perfect 24 hours'. I was still befuddled. So I started with the opposite: What kind of 24 hours did I absolutely NOT want? That was easier.

After that, I was able to open my mind and imagine a truly incredible lifestyle. Thinking that it was merely fantasy, I allowed myself to go wild.

Over a decade later, I found myself living what felt like a perfect 24 hours several times. It took dozens of vision boards, roadmaps, planners, and ongoing conversations with myself to get to a place that once seemed like a fantasy but now feels very real.

It all starts with your imagination. No matter where you are in life, you are never stuck. Life is truly within your grasp, you just gotta get in the driver's seat and steer.

Leila Hanaumi

"Build meaningful connections. It has been so important to me to surround myself with positive and supportive people who believe in me. This has shown me I am capable of anything and you are, too."

Jacob Taylor
Champion of Change

I am a Deaf teenager born to hearing parents. My mom and I work together to help support other hearing parents with deaf children because it can be confusing how to best help their kids.

We work together to raise awareness and teach basic ASL on Instagram, and I teach an Introduction to ASL class.

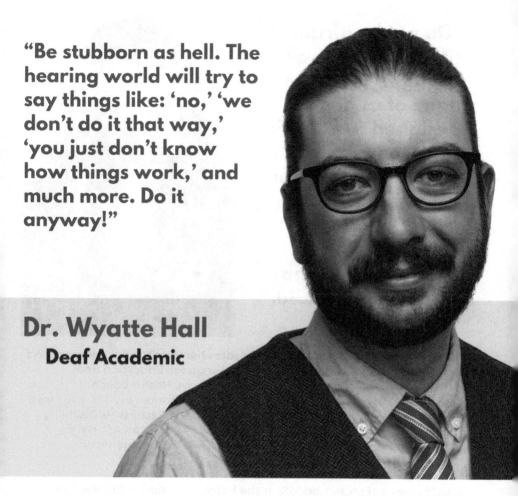

> "Be stubborn as hell. The hearing world will try to say things like: 'no,' 'we don't do it that way,' 'you just don't know how things work,' and much more. Do it anyway!"

Dr. Wyatte Hall
Deaf Academic

I was born deaf in a hearing family. I grew up mainstreamed using an FM system, hearing aids, and sign language interpreters. I went to RIT for my undergraduate degree in Psychology and Gallaudet University for my Ph.D in Clinical Psychology. Through my mainstream experiences and my clinical work, I became interested in understanding, documenting, and researching "language deprivation," both to document its impact on deaf communities and to increase awareness and priority in early intervention systems.

I am faculty in the Public Health Sciences department and direct the Visual Language Access and Acquisition Lab at the University of Rochester Medical Center. I routinely write, present, and publish about the role of early childhood language experiences on quality of life outcomes across the lifespan in deaf populations. I also regularly support other deaf academics ranging from graduate to faculty level across the country to increase the number of deaf people in STEM and allied fields.

> **"Do not be afraid to fit out. All of us are trying to fit in, but none of us are designed to fit in. Find something that sparks your joy and keeps you going. Grasp onto that."**

Allison Friedman
Spiritual Health Coach and Actress

Allison Friedman is passionate and devotes her time to education, art, and advocacy. Allison earned her MA in Sign Language Education from Gallaudet University and received her Integrative Health Coach Certification from the Institute for Integrative Nutrition. In 2023, she was a finalist for the Awareness Campaign Award at the Easterseals Disability Film Festival with the short film **They**, and she also did an ASL national anthem performance at the Chicago Bears' NFL football game on Christmas Eve of 2022.

Allison gave a TEDx talk on "ASL is the Essence of Human Connection." Allison has been an advocate for Deaf children to have access to language from birth and ending language deprivation. She also engages in a Deaf mentoring program for some families and co-chaired LEAD-K (Language Equality and Acquisition for Deaf Kids) in Illinois, where she was born and raised.

Allison is the owner of Sharing My Noga, a service-based business that offers holistic health coaching and online courses. Sharing My Noga's mission is to help her clients rediscover the light inside them. She has a course at Deaf Academy, "How to Embrace Your Spiritual Journey: The Stages of Spiritual Awakening." Allison aims to help others seek a healthy lifestyle to create a more loving world.

www.sharingmynoga.teachable.com/p/home

"When you have **PASSION**, you in fact **SUCCEED** at what you are doing and fulfill your **DREAMS!**"

Melissa Kate Adams-Silva (MK) and Adam Silva
Ying Yang Duo

We were both raised in the New England area and met at NTID/RIT. We have a love for sharing and connecting with others while also showing the world that DEAF CAN DO ANYTHING.

We now have four children whom we have homeschooled from day one. Our passion for creating home remedies and custom designs stems from our passion to care for others and provide something that is helpful for all, as well as unique and fits each individual's needs.

www.802littlehandsbighands.com

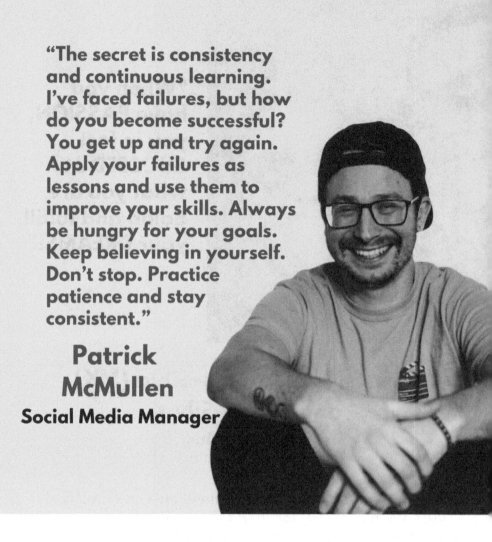

"The secret is consistency and continuous learning. I've faced failures, but how do you become successful? You get up and try again. Apply your failures as lessons and use them to improve your skills. Always be hungry for your goals. Keep believing in yourself. Don't stop. Practice patience and stay consistent."

Patrick McMullen
Social Media Manager

I am a social media creator who has grown to 1 million followers on TikTok. I also run a business where I consult businesses and individuals on how to grow on social media.

Additionally, I manage influencers. I have a passion for the social media space because I truly believe that deaf creators can be as successful as hearing people.

www.instagram.com/thepatrickmcmullen

> **"No one understands your dream; you have to show it to the world. It is only when you turn a dream into reality that others can learn and turn their own dreams into reality."**

Antonia Venesse Guy
Astrologer

Antonia Venesse Guy is the first Deaf and DeafBlind certified professional astrologer and teacher with a passion for her work. She has devoted over 15 years to mastering her craft. Astro Woke offers a range of services, including classes, workshops, and consultations, all conducted in sign language to ensure accessibility for the Deaf community. As an advocate, she is sharing the awareness of Protactile language for the DeafBlind community, which brings deep connections that we all create together in the universe. This initiative reflects her deep sense of inclusivity and her desire to make her expertise available to a wider audience.

In addition to her astrological work, Antonia offers clairvoyant abilities through 1:1 readings, further sharing her spiritual gifts and dedication to helping others navigate life's aspects. Antonia Guy's journey is defined by her dedication to her astrological profession and spiritual journey, her commitment to accessibility, and her vibrant personal interests.

www.astrowoke.com

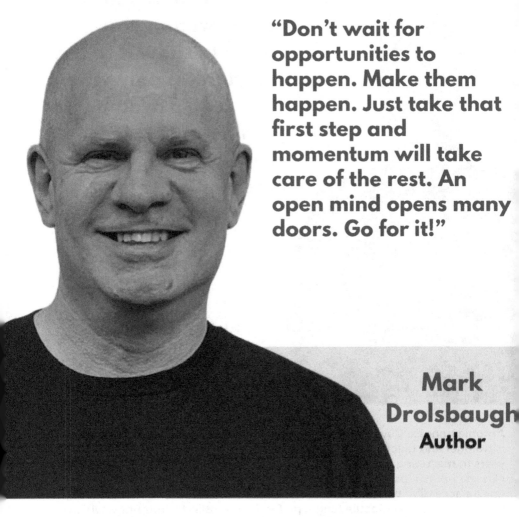

> "Don't wait for opportunities to happen. Make them happen. Just take that first step and momentum will take care of the rest. An open mind opens many doors. Go for it!"

Mark Drolsbaugh
Author

Mark Drolsbaugh has written several deaf-related books, including **Anything But Silent, Deaf Again, On the Fence, and Madness in the Mainstream.** After being told he was "too quiet," he wrote a loud book about introverts, **People Suck, A Cheat Code for Introverts.** Now he calls himself a deaftrovert.

He'll advocate passionately for something and then disappear for months at a time. Follow him on Twitter (if he shows up) at @DrolzUncensored.

www.handwavepublications.com

"Don't be afraid to speak up and share your perspective, even if it takes courage to be the only voice in the room."

Sheila Xu
Pilot and Aspiring Astronaut

Sheila is an oral and signing deaf woman who aspires to be a deaf astronaut. She has earned her concurrent Master's degrees in Public Policy and Business Administration from Harvard and Wharton (2024), and holds a Bachelor of Science degree in Earth, Atmospheric, and Planetary Sciences and Science, Technology, and Society from the Massachusetts Institute of Technology (2014).

Sheila authored a Wharton case study on disability and human space exploration and completed a Harvard Master's thesis on improving accessibility of human spaceflights for deaf and hard of hearing astronauts. Sheila is an Ambassador and Deputy Director of Development at AstroAccess, a nonprofit organization advancing disability inclusion in the space sector. Sheila and her deaf and hard of hearing crew members conducted American Sign Language legibility experiments in zero gravity during a Zero-G parabolic flight. This trailblazing work, part of AstroAccess's mission, aims to explore how space vessels can be made accessible for astronauts with disabilities.

After making history as one of the first deaf commercial analog astronaut trainees at BioSphere2/University of Arizona and as the first deaf Asian female pilot, she's on a mission to champion for inclusion of astronauts with disabilities in human space exploration missions.

www.sheilaxu.com

"You will never know if you don't try...
Seize the opportunity and go for it! If it
doesn't work, then regroup and try
something different. Have confidence
and believe in yourself.

Ignore the naysayers – who cares what
they think? It's not about them, it's about
you. It won't always be easy, so
surround yourself with people who
believe in you. They will be your
cheerleaders, pick you up when you fall,
laugh and cry with you, and push you
when you need it.

Explore, experiment, and try different
things until you find what feels right.
Listen to your gut. Stay curious and keep
learning because you can do anything!"

Karla Giese

Karla Giese
Dr. G: Always Learning!

For Karla, deaf education has been a way of life. Born hearing, Karla began losing her hearing as an infant and became profoundly deaf as a toddler. Her parents chose to raise her with an emphasis on spoken language, using speech therapy, hearing aids, and FM systems while being educated in the mainstream setting. By middle school, Karla began learning sign language and used an interpreter through high school and college. In college, Karla discovered the Deaf community and ASL. After many years of teaching in a variety of total communication programs, Karla learned about Cued Speech and its benefits. Her philosophy is that there is no one deaf experience. She is passionate about effective communication and equitable access within the home, school, and community for Deaf, DeafBlind, and Hard of Hearing children, youth, and adults.

Currently working in the field of learning and development and instructional design, Dr. Karla Giese has served in a variety of roles. Karla's background in Deaf Education as an instructor, administrator, educational consultant, and Deaf advocate puts her in a unique position to provide professional development trainings and online learning on numerous Deaf Awareness and Accessibility topics. Throughout her career, Karla has worked with Deaf and Hard of Hearing people of all ages, from birth to age 21, across all educational settings, utilizing all communication approaches. It's been a great learning experience that has contributed to her own personal growth and identity. Karla is personally and professionally active in the Deaf Community and enjoys sharing her experiences with others.

In her free time, she enjoys reading, spending time with her family, and attending her kid's sports events and activities.

Yeh Kim
YESPAL Creator

"Invest in your favorite hobbies with any money you make or save up. It's okay to have multiple interests – they can merge and fuel your passion and success!"

As a Deaf Seoul-native American (he/they), I am passionate about traveling and sharing my experiences with the global Deaf community. My intersectional perspective allows me to offer insightful tour guides and knowledge about Korea, Korean Sign Language, and East Asian systems. I hold three MA degrees: Professional Studies in Deaf Education and Human Resources Development from RIT, Sign Language Education from Gallaudet University, and Linguistics from Gallaudet University.

As a freelancing expat and content creator, I enjoy documenting my Korean-American journey and unique discoveries. I also founded the first Deaf Korean entrepreneurship, providing tour guides in South Korea and collaborating on projects that serve the South Korean Deaf community. My current goal is to promote and heal Korean Sign Language.

www.yespalbiz.com

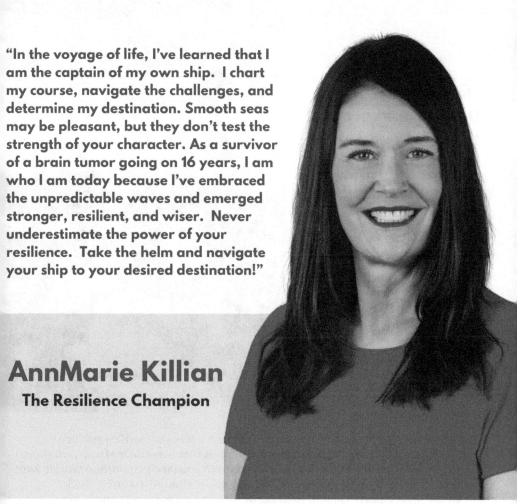

"In the voyage of life, I've learned that I am the captain of my own ship. I chart my course, navigate the challenges, and determine my destination. Smooth seas may be pleasant, but they don't test the strength of your character. As a survivor of a brain tumor going on 16 years, I am who I am today because I've embraced the unpredictable waves and emerged stronger, resilient, and wiser. Never underestimate the power of your resilience. Take the helm and navigate your ship to your desired destination!"

AnnMarie Killian
The Resilience Champion

AnnMarie's role as the CEO of TDIforAccess, Inc., and her commitment to fostering accessibility and inclusion for information and communication technology is commendable. Her extensive two decades of experience in the telecommunications industry undoubtedly provide her with valuable insights and expertise in this field.

Additionally, her involvement as a Co-Founder and board member of the Sho Sum Luv Foundation (SSLF) highlights her dedication to making a positive impact beyond her professional endeavors. AnnMarie's reputation for transforming life's challenges into opportunities is a testament to her resilience and determination, which undoubtedly contribute to her success in her mission.

> "Go out and meet Deaf people around the world and share their stories in their own sign languages for our future generations."

Joel Barish
DeafNation CEO and World Adventurer

Joel Barish is an adventurer and advocate who has visited 103+ nations worldwide to live the Deaf experience. He has discovered Deaf individuals in every hidden corner of the world and shared thousands of unique stories with others through sign language videos and social media channels. Joel is invested in supporting local Deaf communities in his travels and videos, working with local tourism offices to help increase awareness and accessibility for traveling Deaf individuals.

Joel is the co-founder of DeafNation Expo, the world's premier business serving the Deaf community with over a million attendees since 2003. The acclaimed No Barriers with Joel Barish is an inspiring, adventurous travelogue in Sign Language that allows viewers to join Joel as he tastes unique cuisine, meets inspirational Deaf business owners, and explains the significance of various landmarks he travels to. Notable episodes include going 6,500 feet under the earth to mine gold with a Deaf South African gold miner and hunting for survival while boating with Deaf native Inuit in Greenland.

Coffee With Joel Barish is a talk show where Joel interviews notable Deaf people on a variety of topics. Joel's guests include leaders, politicians, and individuals with interesting professions or experiences, and cover topics that are interesting and relevant to the Deaf and signing community. In his spare time, Joel enjoys cycling, photography, and spending time with his family.

www.deafnation.com

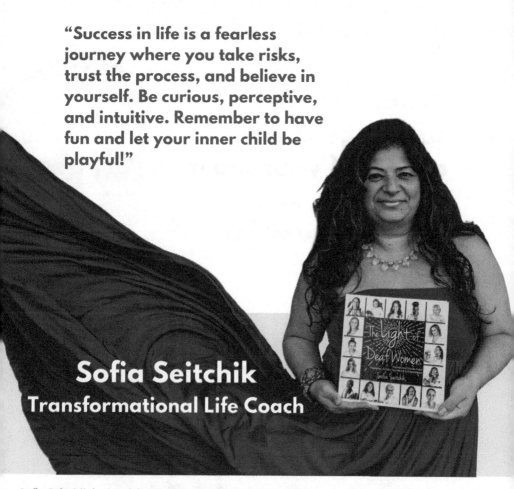

"Success in life is a fearless journey where you take risks, trust the process, and believe in yourself. Be curious, perceptive, and intuitive. Remember to have fun and let your inner child be playful!"

Sofia Seitchik
Transformational Life Coach

Sofia Seitchik is the visionary founder of Global Deaf Women, a transformative coaching service that has inspired and empowered hundreds of Deaf women entrepreneurs to transform their lives from the inside out. She is the author of the award-winning book **The Light of Deaf Women: Inspirational Stories From Visionaries, Artists, Founders & Entrepreneurs**.

Sofia is also a sought-after speaker, sharing her insights on a range of topics, including her journey as a Jewish Deaf woman, women's empowerment, and the power of mindset transformation. Born in Samarkand, Uzbekistan, and raised in St. Petersburg, Russia (formerly the Soviet Union), Sofia immigrated to the United States with her family as a teenager.

One of her most cherished adventures was traveling to 20 countries over seven months with her family, during which she and her husband homeschooled their two sons. Sofia graduated from Gallaudet University and served as the Program Director for the Jewish Deaf Congress, playing a pivotal role in revitalizing the organization. She currently works part-time as a Program Director at Gallaudet University for Hillel.

www.globaldeafwomen.com

"Your ego will sabotage every aspect of your life if you don't set it aside and ask for help."

Christopher "Salt" Morton

Inspirational Speaker

Christopher "Salt" Morton is the first Deaf man who embarked on a 235-day journey walking across America alone with no prior camping/hiking experience. He was able to absorb life in a way he never thought imaginable.

He's been able to use his experiences to further develop his "V.I.T.A.L" presentations that have allowed him to transform himself from someone that sabotaged his own happiness to becoming someone that was able to find purpose in his life.

He continues to contribute back to society by providing speeches across the country on subjects necessary for others to unlock their potential and overcome their fear of failure.

"Deaf Latino CAN DO IT."

Juan Bernal
Latino Deaf Activist

Juan was born in San Luis Potosi, Mexico. Juan has three beautiful Deaf children and two grandsons. Juan is the winner of the Deaf Illinois Award 2013 and the current holder of the Best Deaf Activist title.

Juan is president of the National Hispanic Latino Association of the Deaf and co-founder of the Illinois Deaf Latino Association. Juan also works as an LSM Deaf Interpreter.

"Surround yourself with people who share your passion. Choose your life's work based on your passion. Passion fuels success and when your day-to-day work is your passion, you won't feel like you are working."

Karen Hopkins

Executive Director of The Children's Center for Communication/Beverly School for the Deaf

Dr. Karen Hopkins is the Executive Director of The Children's Center for Communication/Beverly School for the Deaf. She brings over 33 years of experience as a collaborative teacher of the deaf, special educator, early interventionist, grant writer, and educational administrator to her work with Deaf and hard of hearing children. Her work with families, coupled with her own personal experience as a Deaf adult and parent of a daughter who is hard of hearing have inspired her to create systems that empower families. Karen oversees early intervention and educational programming for children and young adults who are Deaf or hard of hearing from birth to age 22 in the North Shore of Massachusetts.

She is active in many organizations and boards, is the current President of the Hands & Voices HQ Board of Directors, and is involved with international FCEI programming including the Deaf Leadership International Alliance. Karen has presented throughout the United States, Austria, and China on supporting families who have deaf and hard of hearing children. Karen's current research is focused on perspectives of family empowerment in early intervention systems for Deaf and hard of hearing children.

"My 6-year old daughter once told me that if I don't play with her, she won't be happy. I told her that we can play tomorrow. 'But tomorrow is not promised,' she shot back with a sad look on her face, followed by a tight bear hug. She reminded me what I've been preaching for many years... Life is too short. Opportunity for success does disappear before you blink your eyes. If you're passionate about anything, go for it as if there's no tomorrow."

Earl Allen
Advocate

Earl Allen was born and raised in Washington D.C., not far from the nation's Capitol. Earl became deaf at the age of three and attended Kendall Demonstration Elementary School and graduated from Model Secondary School for the Deaf. Earl earned his B.A. degree in Criminology from Gallaudet University. Earl has worked several odd jobs, including a brief return to graduate school at Gallaudet before landing a full-time career with the United States government in the City of Brotherly Love – Philadelphia, Pennsylvania.

After eight years of serving America's taxpayers, Earl relocated to Rochester, New York, worked four years at the National Technical Institute for the Deaf and is currently employed at the University of Rochester. Earl enjoys spending time with his wife and daughter, bowling in a league, and playing cards with friends.

"Historically, success meant just surviving in my opinion. If I survived the day I was successful. That was when I was five years old and did not have much to really worry about. Now, success means something different, for me it means finding a balance between work and living my life.

Each one of us experiences a different journey through life. I think it helps if we identify where we have passion. What do you enjoy? You only find what you enjoy by trying different things. Next, can you set achievable goals and do what you enjoy? This creates a sense of accomplishment and a feeling of making progress in life. Are you willing to take action toward those goals even if it means failing? I hate failing, with a passion. It feels so uncomfortable and even painful when I feel like I have failed at something. But my theory of failure is different from others. What I might see as failing is what someone else may see as success. When I feel like I am failing I try to look at things from a different perspective and I try to figure out how I can move on even while feeling uncomfortable. Can I introduce my passion into getting through what I see as failure? Doing that while staying positive is hard, and by no means am I an expert.

For me it helps to recognize that we all have ups and downs, but we truly only experience our ups and downs. We can either get through the ups and downs as our own worst enemy or as a comforting friend. Which would you prefer?"

Tony Abou Ezzi

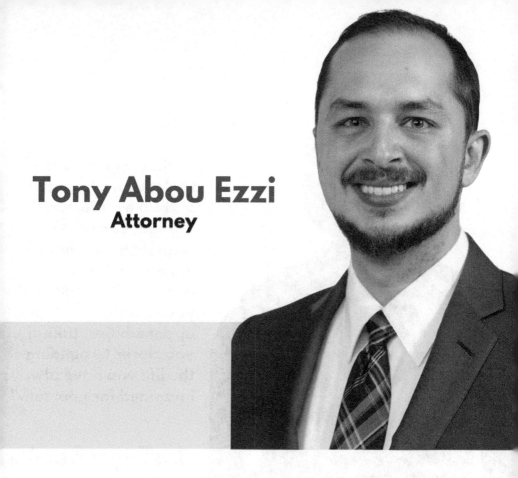

Tony Abou Ezzi
Attorney

I am the owner of Ezzi Law. I represent families through some of life's most difficult circumstances. I work with my clients to navigate Estate Planning, Personal Injury (nursing home abuse, medical malpractice, wrongful death), Guardianship and Probate (decedent's estates).

I have a bilateral moderate-to-severe hearing loss and throughout my early education, I witnessed and experienced many issues faced by individuals with a disability and the elderly. Ranging from lack of appropriate accommodations to outright physical and mental abuse, I first discovered my passion for advocating for others back in high school while volunteering with the elderly in nursing homes and having to engage in my own self-advocacy.

I am the President of the Arab American Bar Association of Illinois, and a participant in the Justice Entrepreneurs Project in Chicago.

"Align yourself with people who are doing exactly what you want to do. Learn from them and take opportunities offered, even if it is something you never would do. Those opportunities will lead you to other opportunities, taking you closer to building the life you have always imagined for yourself."

LaToya Banks
Educator and Advocate

LaToya Banks is an educator, advocate, and aspiring writer who identifies as deaf. Her days are spent educating children who are deaf/HOH/deaf plus, and their parents, hoping to make a difference one family at a time. In addition, LaToya continues to grow in her advocacy for children who are on the autism spectrum. Guiding families, sharing resources, and building community.

Aside from her life's work, she enjoys writing during her spare time – hoping to publish a book about her own journey as well as children's books. Books she wishes existed for her when she was a young girl. Her spare time is spent listening to music, traveling, reading, writing, and venturing to explore all that her native city has to offer.

> "You can't decide in advance if you're going to be successful at something. You have to actually take the action to do it, and just let it unfold – one step at a time."

Eric Epstein

ASL Poet

Eric is an ASL poet whose work has been featured in the Folger Shakespeare Library traveling exhibition and the Rail Switch journal. He has taught sign language poetics and translation through several workshops at four different colleges. Additionally, he has coached and mentored Deaf performers as well as professional sign language interpreters so that they would win top honors in various national competitions.

He currently produces ASL translations of English poems, which have been commissioned by English-language poets from all over the country — such as the poet laureate of Missouri. His groundbreaking curriculum in the signing arts can be found on Signplaying.com, which has been used by various signing instructors for their ASL classes at Boise State University, Rochester Institute of Technology, and an international training program for signing artists in Sweden-based theatre Riksteatern Crea.

www.signplaying.com

"Living life successfully and with passion would include finding an interest, developing meaningful relationships, hard work, determination, and resilience. If you have intersecting identities, it is important to be aware of the additional challenges. For example, as a Black Deaf woman, I am aware that I have additional challenges due to the intersection of gender, race, and deafness. Having a strong support system that includes friends, family, and those in the professional arena is very important. Professional connections are also important and if they fall within any of the intersecting identities, that's a rare gem. Pursuing an education or establishing career goals that are in alignment with your passion and/or your success is also critical. Advocacy skills are needed because of intersecting identities – you will have to fight for accessibility, equal opportunities, and representation. Connecting with Deaf and Black or the Black Deaf community is important to provide that sense of belonging and to stay empowered. Finally, for passion, it is important to engage in hobbies and interests that you are passionate about and it brings joy or makes your soul feel alive. Happiness comes from within, and I think pursuing something with a purpose and determination while focusing on your strengths will keep the passion alive."

Dr. Alesia Allen

Dr. Alesia Allen

**VP of
Diversity and Inclusion**

Alesia Allen, Ph.D, is the Assistant Vice President of the Office of Diversity and Inclusion at the National Technical Institute for the Deaf (NTID) on the Rochester Institute of Technology (RIT) campus. In this role, she monitors diversity, inclusion, equal opportunity, access regulations, issues in higher education, and advises the president and other NTID administrators on matters related to diversity and inclusion. Additionally, she ensures accessibility and inclusive collaboration while bridging gaps between NTID and university-wide initiatives at RIT.

Dr. Allen has more than 15 years of professional, clinical, and teaching experience, and she worked on several initiatives to promote system changes that impact deaf and hard of hearing individuals who come from diverse backgrounds. Her career included providing therapy and assessments to deaf and hard of hearing individuals, clinical consultations, teaching, and advocating for better mental health services for this population. Prior to becoming the AVP, she served as a visiting assistant professor in NTID's Department of Liberal Studies where she taught a variety of courses in Psychology as well as engaging in scholarship, mentoring students, and serving on several committees. Dr. Allen holds a Doctoral and a Master's degree in Clinical Psychology from Gallaudet University and a Bachelor's in Psychology from RIT. In her spare time, she enjoys traveling and spending time with her family.

CJ Jones

"When you believe in yourself, anything is possible. I believed it. You see, my dream came true because I believed in myself. So can you.

In order to reach your destiny, you must have passion and the right attitude.

To ensure your success in life, be ahead of the game.

Once you accept ying and yang as part of your life, you will gain wisdom and compassion.

Persistence is the key to success and patience is the ultimate force of resilience.
Dream with your eyes open: opportunities are all around you. Believe it. Know it.

Wake up with a smile like the sun rises in the horizon, your mind and heart will feel focused, balanced, loved, and nurtured.

When you maintain a positive life, you attract positive people.

Read positive messages – this is your daily vitamin intake.

Life is short – make a bucket list to fulfill your journey. It's your right.

You have every means to be inspired at any time and anywhere you desire to be.

You have the power to make a difference in life, simply activate your purpose.

Laughter is important because your body needs happiness, so make it a habit.

It is nice to have wealth but the most inexpensive and free thing is: HUG.

Be appreciated. I appreciate you.
Be thankful. I thank you.
Be loved. I love you.

Life is good and so are YOU. Namaste!"

CJ Jones

Artist,
Filmmaker, Leader,
Motivational Speaker

CJ Jones is a producer, director, writer, actor, comedian, musician, DASL (Director of Artistic Sign Language), and motivational speaker. CJ is a living legend in the deaf and hearing world, acclaimed for his humor, creativity, and inspiration. He has done it all: TV (A Different World, Everything Gonna Be Okay, Shameless, Castle Rock, Door in the Woods), films (Baby Driver, Avatar), theater and performed internationally as a standup comedian for 50 years. (www.cjjones.com).

CJ founded SignWorld Studios (www.signworldstudios.com) and SignLight, a nonprofit organization, with its mission to create a film training program for the Deaf and Hard of Hearing (www.signlight.org). He is the producer of the SignLight International Film Festival.

CJ Jones received KCET/Los Angeles Local Hero of the Year Award 2008 in Celebration of Black History Month, NAD Breakthrough Awards 2017, SAG-AFTRA Harold Russell Award by Media Access Awards 2018, and a honorary degree from Gallaudet University 2020-2021.

www.cjjones.com

"You won't be able to succeed at anything until you fail at something, learn from your mistake, and never make the same mistake again. Patience is the key to success. It is never too late to make your dream come true, no matter how old you are! Always balance your life and career stability; especially, your health comes first. Number one thing you should do is, never listen to those people who don't want you to succeed in life. They hate that, always focus on the important people in your lives that support YOU."

Justin Loncar
somedeafguy

Justin Loncar, also known as somedeafguy. He's not your average comedian; he's a laughter maestro. With his uproarious social media skits and stand-up performances, Justin is on a mission to share the joy of laughter with the world.

He's the face of Our Stage Vodka. It's not just a drink; it's a symbol of togetherness. Justin's deep connection with this unique vodka brand represents the power of shared stages, shared laughter, and the incredible sense of unity it brings.

www.instagram.com/somedeafguy_ (Note: include the underscore.)

"DO IT WITH PASSION OR NOTHING AT ALL!"

Sara Smania
Business Owner

Sara Smania is a vibrant soul being, hailing from a 5th-generation deaf family. She along with her partner run "House of All Trades," which offers various services such as cleaning, lawn service, small home repairs, painting, and other services.

In her free time, Sara finds solace in exploring the world through hiking and nature. Sara's infectious positivity and passion for life shine through her daily quotes inspiring others to embrace their own journeys and appreciate the beauty of life.

Garrett Scott

"Don't give up on your dreams of success. You'll start at a rookie level, but as you gain more experience and expertise, you'll face challenges that will help you discover new ways to learn and grow. You'll find new goals to strive for and never stop improving. With persistence and dedication, you'll become more renowned and accomplished in your field, and your success will be a testament to your hard work and determination."

Garrett Scott
The Deaf Grappler

My name is Garrett Scott, I am Deaf, and I am the first Deaf American to hold a black belt in Brazilian Jiu Jitsu – in both the Brazilian Jiu Jitsu community and Deaf community.

I am a professional grappler and professional mixed martial artist and MMA/BJJ instructor. I am a 4x World Deaf Jiu Jitsu champion, plus I won multiple championships in Brazilian Jiu Jitsu and Grappling.

Marianne Jodie Grote

Data Analyst

Marianne's full-time role as a wife, caregiver, and a bonus mom speaks volumes, balancing work as a career woman and a partner in crime with Charlie. Marianne's passion for data insights is a driving force in her professional and personal life.

With over 15 years of diverse experience in HR, Media Planning, and Marketing, she brings a unique perspective to her role as a Senior Analyst of Equal Opportunity/Affirmative Action at Walgreens, an integrated healthcare, pharmacy, and retail leader. She builds efficient tools for key stakeholders and leaders to strategize their goals for women, people of color/minorities, people with disabilities, and veterans.

She received an MBA in Marketing from the University of Arizona and a post-graduate certificate in Business Analytics. Her hobbies include walking Bailey, a rescued Puerto Rican smooth fox terrier/pointer dog with Charlie, yoga, sprint triathlons, and she's a traveling adventurer.

"Allyship builds the foundation for increased opportunities. Allyship is a two-way street that allows mutual respect and trust in life to share wisdom. You acquire exceptional skills and provide what the company needs – they see you as an asset. The person who sees you with the capabilities, not the disability, is an ally.

The knowledge you bring to the table and a seat in the boardroom and with leaders bring awareness and collaboration for others to see YOUR value. Knowledge is the key to open opportunities.

Be searching for Allies. Be authentic. Be persistent. Be ambitious. Be transparent. Challenge yourself to learn new tools. Be proud of yourself for what you accomplish in life. Be an interesting person. Be kind. Be willing to speak up. Be a good listener/observer. Be empathic. Be thankful. Stay away from toxic people. Do not gossip. Gossip wastes life. Enjoy and have fun in life."

Marianne Jodie Grote

> "The more one glows and shines, others follow, resulting in a sweeping illuminating effect exponentially!"

Charles Wildbank
Artist

Charles Bourke Wildbank, native Long Island photorealism artist, holds degrees from Pratt and Columbia Universities in New York. He paints large canvases spanning several themes: portraits, seascapes, florals, still life and portraiture.

One of Wildbank's major works available for viewing would be his large mural commissions with Cunard Line for the Queen Mary 2 cruise ship. His art is included in several corporate art collections and has been displayed in such notable locations as Cartier, Rome's Hassler Hotel (Deaf owner, Roberto Wirth RIP) and Rockefeller Center offices. To this day, he conducts painting workshops throughout USA and Europe, and is available for exhibitions, art presentations, charity functions and studio tours.

"With each brush stroke I strive to reveal the essence and innate beauty of the subject, whether it be the rhythmic waves across the surface of the sea or the gentle contours and subtleties of faces in my portraitures."

www.wildbank.com

Painting by Charles Wildbank

"Bet on yourself and don't ever give up.

Be yourself, there's no one better.

Stay busy and be useful."

Patti Sánchez
Employment Consultant

A Brooklyn, New York native born to mainland Puerto Rican parents, Patti is Deaf and a Certified Career Coach. Patti received an MBA with a concentration in Human Resources from the University of Phoenix.

She provides diversity training skills to corporations to educate them about Deaf culture and accommodations when hiring a Deaf individual. She is a content creator for the ASL Employment Curriculum on YouTube. She's the author of Breaking Barriers: Effective Strategies and Creating an Inclusive Workplace for Deaf and Hard of Hearing Job Seekers. Patti also writes articles for the ASDC Endeavor and holds a certificate in Diversity, Equity, and Inclusion (DEI).

In her spare time, she enjoys spending time with her family and friends, attending Latin music concerts, and traveling. She has a dog named Luna.

> "To be your best self, get rid of conditions that don't serve you. Instead, nurture those conditions that do serve you. There is no need to create another version of yourself. Simply be true to yourself."

Diana Cho
Life Coach

Diana Cho, BA, BS, MS, is a life coach, and has been a program administrator, supervisor, advocate, and facilitator.

At the Rochester Institute of Technology, she served as a departmental and program administrator as well as a staff and student supervisor. She implemented, delivered, and taught curriculum and service programs, and was an admissions counselor. While at the Vera Institute of Justice, Diana worked to improve services for women with disabilities and Deaf women who have experienced violence. She has also served as a meeting facilitator with several national nonprofit organizations, and has volunteered for countless community activities.

Diana is Deaf. She finds pleasure in creating artwork, hiking in nature, and spending time with animals

www.dianacho.com

instagram.com/coach.dianacho

"To embrace a life of passion and success, cultivate a growth mindset, surround yourself with positivity, and set clear goals that you regularly revisit. Stepping outside your comfort zone builds confidence and fuels your drive to thrive. Develop both short- and long-term goals, and when setbacks occur, rise resiliently. Treat every experience as a chance to learn. Hold onto your dreams steadfastly, and believe in them unwaveringly. Recognize the vital connection between preparation, planning, and the pursuit of passion and success.

Did you know that persistence is the fuel for dreams? Wondering how to persist in the face of challenges? Maintain your passion for your dreams, wants, and desires. What keeps you moving forward despite setbacks is a relentless belief in your dreams and persistent effort. If setbacks occur, rise again, keeping the flame of passion alive. Remember these four principles:

Align your passion with your dreams!
Align your dreams with persistence!
Understand that setbacks are part of the journey; rise again and start anew.
Stay focused and never let go of your dreams."

Latisha Porter Vaughn

Latisha's own journey began with a challenge. She discovered she had been born with sensorineural hearing loss at the age of 19, but she didn't let it define her. She took on the world, armed with determination and a heart full of compassion.

Today, Latisha is the President of the HLAA New Jersey State Association, a scholarship chair, and the co-founder of the HLAA Essex County Chapter. But her story doesn't end there. She's also recently earned her Ph.D in Organizational Development and Leadership, focusing on Perceptions of Deaf and Hard-of-Hearing College Students' Work Readiness and Preparation.

Latisha Porter Vaughn
Author and Advocate

Latisha's life is an incredible example of perseverance, advocacy, and hard work. She was born with hearing loss, uses hearing aids, reads lips, and utilizes assistive listening devices. Her goal is to promote inclusivity, and her research contributes to that vision. Latisha previously worked as a Research Associate for the National Deaf Center, where she assisted institutions in supporting deaf students.

But it's not just her professional work that makes her a HearStrong Champion. She's also the author of "Sounds of the Heart: A Story of a HearStrong Champion Persisting Against All Odds." In addition, she's written two other books, "Whispered Journeys: Spoken Softly but Loudly Understood," and "Hearing Loss: A Useful Guide for the Hearing," which offers practical advice and solutions for hearing loss in the workplace, public settings, and social situations.

Latisha has been employed at Seton Hall Law School for over 30 years and is dedicated to creating a culture of hearing loss awareness. Her work has touched countless lives in her community, and it's time for her impact to reach even further.

Diamond Powell
Future Teacher and Author

"No one has so much power over you except you. Who's gonna stop you from being so dope? Nobody. The answer will always be, nobody."

Diamond Shajazz Powell was born and raised in Baltimore, MD. She became Deaf at the age of five and attended mainstream schools in upstate New York. Diamond is currently studying at NTID for her Master's in Secondary Education for students who are Deaf and Hard of Hearing.

Her greatest passions are writing and education. She has written poetry and has been published two years in a row (2021 & 2022) in RIT's literary magazine, **Signatures**. She enjoys reading and writing fantasy in her free time.

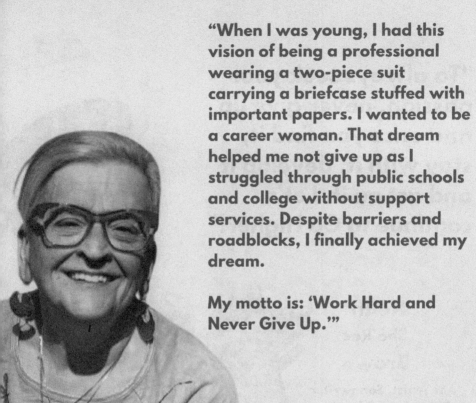

"When I was young, I had this vision of being a professional wearing a two-piece suit carrying a briefcase stuffed with important papers. I wanted to be a career woman. That dream helped me not give up as I struggled through public schools and college without support services. Despite barriers and roadblocks, I finally achieved my dream.

My motto is: 'Work Hard and Never Give Up.'"

Solange "Sally" Skyer
Artist

Retired academic advisor, counselor, and associate professor at NTID/RIT. Worked at NTID for 38 years.

Mother of two deafened adults. Married to late-deafened husband.

"To always seek your passion, never give up and once you find it, stay with it, develop it and act on it. Let's continue to Go Higher!"

Keith
Sho'Roc
Brown

ASL Artist, Songwriter, Actor, Deaf Advocacy, Motivational Speaker

Sho'Roc was born in Wilmington, Delaware and later moved to Washington D.C., where he begin his journey as a musician. He was inspired to become a recording artist when he met a deaf rapper named Prinz-D at Gallaudet University.

Sho'Roc and Prinz-D formed the first deaf Hip-Hop group called Helix Boyz with one album completed. He also got his first acting role (Gab) in Hip-Hop Anansi by Eisa Davis at the Imagination Stage Theatre in 2006.

Sho'Roc has collaborated with WaWa's World and DJ Nicar on various projects such as "We No Hear" and "Random Thoughts," and recorded songs with Beautiful the Artist (song called "Always Up") and CODA rappers Orel B Tha Coda and J. Cacao. He released his first solo album called "Triple Threat" in 2021 with hit single "Go Higher" and "W.U.M.B.," produced by DJ Nicar.

www.instagram.com/sho.roc

"My advice for deaf, deaf-blind and hard of hearing people:
You will face hard obstacles daily, but you will get through and have success in your life! Just keep doing what you love with passion and you will succeed at what you love to do!"

Haylie Brandt-Ogle
Future Psychologist

I'm deaf-blind. I have Usher Syndrome Type 1B. I'm also currently in college, majoring in Psychology to become a clinical psychologist.

I am Vice-President of the Silent Bucs club, and I love to inspire others knowing that they will be able to feel connected.

> "If you're passionate about something, don't give up. Be persistent and patient, because success takes time. Practice your skills and gain experience, network and get advice from mentors. No matter where you are in your career, never stop learning."

Melinda Schallau
Seasoned Graphic Designer

Profoundly deaf since birth, I had a great deal of imagination growing up. Art has always fascinated me because it allows me to have creative freedom to express myself. I became interested in pursuing a career in Graphic Design after I discovered it sparked my passion to tell a story through visual communication, and I loved being creative.

I graduated from NTID/RIT with a Bachelor of Fine Arts (BFA) in Graphic Design in 2005.

For the past 18 years in Austin, I worked at QuantumDigital and WildKind Packaging, which gave me extensive experience in print design that includes direct mail and packaging design.

Later this year, I plan to pursue my dream of becoming a full-time freelance graphic designer and starting my own studio business. As an AIGA member, I enjoy connecting and networking with other creatives. I was a Creative Mass Chair at AIGA Austin Chapter for a year to help host social events for creatives and was featured in AIGA Houston Chapter for Deaf Awareness Month. In addition, I founded Deaf Etiquette on Instagram with a goal to teach hearing people the do's and don'ts on deaf etiquette in the workplace and beyond.

> "The answer you are currently seeking is within you. Take a step back and meditate on what you truly want out of life. Remember, you only have one life. It is up to you to decide how you want to LIVE it."

Sean Cosslett
Psychology Student

I am a fifth-year student studying Psychology at the Rochester Institute of Technology. There was a notion that the statistics proved that, on average, a student would change their majors at least three times. I recalled that I thought I would never change my major. Five years later, four different majors, and now I've finally settled down with Psychology.

As I reflected on the past five years, I was anxious about the future and trying to figure out what I want to do with my life regarding professional and personal goals. Little did I realize that the answer to my doubts had been within myself all along. I had ignored it because I was afraid of exploring the unknown. This was the moment I realized that Psychology was the field I wanted to study, and I have never looked back since then. Be curious, bold, and enjoy every moment life has in store for you. Lastly, always be grateful.

> "We strive not to let the fear of failure hinder us from taking risks in life and believe in sharing our passion that brings joy to us and others."

Tate and Sarah Tullier
Aritst + Entrepreneur Team

Tate and Sarah Tullier are the best of friends, a married duo, and a creative team. Over their 28 years together, they have run a photography business, several clothing ventures including Cosmic Sobbing, and hosted art showcases. Both are graduates of Gallaudet University.

They have lived in DC, NYC, Baton Rouge, and now reside in Austin. Passionate advocates for the deaf community, Tate and Sarah champion living authentic lives through their work and personal endeavors.

www.tatetullierphotography.com + www.cosmicsobbing.com

"Even if you feel you're not sure you're able to do this or don't have the skills yet, try to present yourself and say you can do this. You can figure out how. Sometimes we have to really evaluate each situation. Sometimes you have to play the long game. You have to keep the future in mind. Maybe there is something you can tolerate for the short term, and not complain about, but eventually you will be able to stand up and advocate for yourself later."

Michael L. Epstein
**Graphic Designer
for Hollywood TV and Movies**

Michael L. Epstein was a Deaf graphic designer who created graphics for AMC, CBS, MTV, NBC, TNT, USA, VH1, Disney, FreeForm, Lucasfilm, Microsoft, Netflix, Showtime, Universal Pictures, and Warner Bros. Pictures. He was known for working in famous TV shows and movies like "The Mandalorian" (2019), "Aquaman" (2018), "The Fate of the Furious" (2017), "Animal Kingdom," and "CSI: Cyber." He was nominated four times for the "Excellence in Production Design" award (given by the Art Directors Guild) for different categories, and he won that award in 2021 for his work in Episode 205 of "The Mandalorian."

At the time of this writing, he is still the only known Deaf person to finally become a member of the IATSE Local 800 (Art Directors Guild). Michael was always an outspoken advocate for the inclusion of Deaf people in the Hollywood industry – particularly focusing on film crew work such as the art department. His tireless advocacy and design work will always be a valuable contribution toward helping other deaf people to become Hollywood crew members. (Michael passed away in 2024).

> "Success is realization of your full potential. Cultivate your aptitude and talent. Let your dharma, calling, and purpose nourish your journey."

Kristen Marie Weiner
AKA Rajarajeshwari
Deaf Yogini

With a keen eye for blending the worlds of Deaf culture and the ancient practice of yoga, Rajarajeshwari has pioneered a unique path that elevates human consciousness through yoga and sign language. Deafhood Yoga® was established in 2010 and answered the powerful vision that emerged in 2008, creating an online yoga studio to inspire, support, and serve kindred hearts of Deaf people and allies from all walks of life. Deafhood Yoga has offered Prenatal Yoga, Children's Yoga, Yoga at Deaf schools and camps, Family Yoga, Adults, Chair Yoga, Elders/Senior Citizens, Private Sessions, Consultations, Beach Yoga, Retreats, and Free CommUnity Yoga.

Deafhood Yoga® was one of the first to explore, build, and continue the concept of an online yoga studio in 2013. In the Fall of 2021, Deafhood Yoga® released its app in the Apple and Google Stores. In 2022, Rajarajeshwari felt called to Isha Hatha Yoga Lineage after learning about it in 2018 and began practicing with them. In 2023, with Isha Hatha Yoga Foundation of Coimbatore, South India, we now offer their yoga sessions in Indian Sign Language and American Sign Language. The journey of Deafhood Yoga® continues, impacting and uplifting the lives of many. Be Yogaself.

www.deafhoodyoga.com

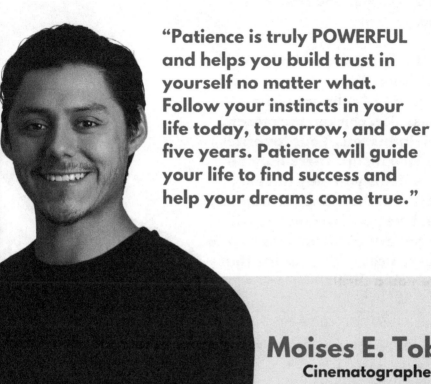

"Patience is truly POWERFUL and helps you build trust in yourself no matter what. Follow your instincts in your life today, tomorrow, and over five years. Patience will guide your life to find success and help your dreams come true."

Moises E. Tobias
Cinematographer and Digital Designer

Moises Ezequiel Tobias is a cinematographer and digital designer. He is a co-founder of Morpheyes Studio (est. 2019) and worked as a Director of Photography for two amazing projects: a short film, INSPIRED (2023), which received nine awards and Deaf Identity, the first documentary episode of Deaf And... (2024), which received three awards.

Moises works as a freelancer – a Digital Designer who has high requirements in digital media including software, 3D animation, motion design, graphic design, UI/UX, editing, digital media, and storyboarding.

Moises graduated from the Rochester Institute of Technology (RIT) in 2023. He will begin studying in a graduate program at the School of Film and Animation at RIT in the fall of 2024.

"Rome wasn't built in a day. Little by little, one step at a time.

Think of passion and success like your favorite restaurant menu. A variety of culinary dishes; moussaka, chicken parmesan, enchiladas, etc. Your favorites are on a menu. There may be some items you may not like, but it's on the menu for others to like. Like passion and success, the options of the menu provide experiences with your life that give you a thrill."

Steven Putz
Mr. Organized Chaos

High-tempo environments are what I love to cater to. Working as a Deaf cook in a predominantly hearing restaurant creates a double layer of chaos for me.

The first layer, is keeping up with the pace of the restaurant and the needs of people. The second layer: communication barriers and overcoming them. Former cook at Cheesecake Factory. Current cook at RIT.

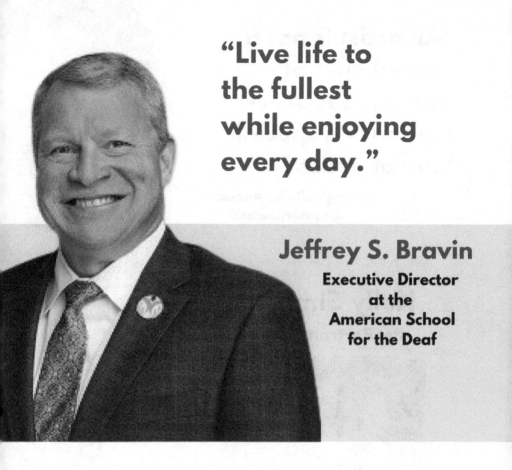

"Live life to the fullest while enjoying every day."

Jeffrey S. Bravin

**Executive Director
at the
American School
for the Deaf**

Jeffrey S. Bravin has been employed at the American School for the Deaf in West Hartford, CT since 2002. He is currently the Executive Director responsible for oversight of the school. Jeffrey earned his B.A. Degree in Government from Gallaudet University, M.S. Degree in Deaf Education from McDaniel College (formerly known as Western Maryland College), and M.S. Degree in School Administration and Supervision from Queens College. He is currently studying for his Ed.D. in Education Leadership at the University of Connecticut.

He also currently serves on the Advisory Board for the State of Connecticut, Department of Aging and Disability Services, the Board of the Connecticut Council on Organizations Serving the Deaf and is the President of the Board of the Conference of Educational Administrators of Schools and Programs for the Deaf (CEASD). He was formerly on the Board of Directors for the National Theatre of the Deaf and American Society of Deaf Children.

www.asd-1817.org

> **"An artist is not a special kind of person, but every person is a special kind of artist."**
>
> ~originally by Ananda Coomaraswami

Kelly Simpson
Pet Portrait Painter

Kelly decided to follow her life's passion and become a full-time artist. In 2009, she started painting animals and doing photography work in her new home, Frederick, MD, after moving from Washington, D.C. and leaving her 19 years as a museum curatorial technician with the federal government.

Kelly's work is in oil on canvas, and has a unique feeling for capturing the pet with their "everyday look" in a contemporary-style against the bright background color...while in the act of painting, she's constantly communicating with the developing image on canvas. Each one has a unique spirit represented in their expressive eyes.

> **"Here are some of my crucial ingredients in life: you are allowed to grow, be assertive, practice good negotiation, and be a better human everyday."**

Lee Ann Tang
Co-Founder and CEO of Asian Signers

Growing up in New Jersey with a signing family, Lee Ann Tang was adopted from Wuxi, China to the United States of America at the age of five where her life forever blossomed with a genuine love and signed language. She proudly graduated from New Jersey School for the Deaf (also known as Marie H. Katzenbach School for the Deaf), where she had rich experiences in playing sports, performance arts, and clubs. She first grasped the Deaf identity because of her father and four Asian siblings who were also adopted. The majority of her family is Deaf, and she also identifies as a Chinese adoptee.

In academics, Lee Ann is an Asian American Deaf educator and a linguist. She currently works as an Assistant Professor in the Department of Deaf Studies at California State University, Northridge (CSUN). Because of American Sign Language, she has always been immersed into languages at a young age which led her to obtain a BA in Deaf Studies from CSUN (2018) and MA in Linguistics from Gallaudet University (2021). She is an advocate for Asian leadership in education.

Additionally, Lee Ann is known for co-founding a nonprofit organization called Asian Signers in early 2020 where she currently serves as the Chief Executive Officer. The organization is Asian-owned, Deaf-led, and non-traditional. It elevates awareness and recognition of diverse Asians and Asian-Americans in Deaf and signing communities, because people of Asian descent are a mosaic and representation does matter. She is forever grateful for continued support from various communities with love.

Holly Jensen

**Money Coach,
Wealth Strategist,
Master IUL Professional**

Holly Parker Jensen was born and raised on a small farm along the Snake River in rural southern Idaho. Holly received her BA degree in Secondary Education/History and an MA degree in Clinical Mental Health Counseling from Gallaudet University with summa cum laude.

Holly's expertise in couples counseling, particularly in alleviating financial tensions, sparked a profound interest in financial empowerment. This passion led her to transition into the finance sector, where she now empowers families to achieve financial freedom and build wealth through innovative alternatives to traditional Wall Street investments.

www.tetonpinesfinancial.com

Unleash Your Inner Entrepreneur: Mastering the Art of Perseverance for Success by Holly Jensen

1. Passion and Purpose:
Allow your passion to kindle a relentless drive within you. With a clearly defined purpose, you are equipped to surmount any obstacle and attain greatness.

2. Set Realistic Goals:
Consider your goals as essential milestones. Celebrate each achievement as a crucial step toward your overarching success.

3. Learn from Setbacks:
View setbacks as invaluable learning opportunities. Each challenge presents a chance to strengthen your resilience and acquire critical insights.

4. Resilience:
Cultivate resilience as if you were nurturing a seed into a sturdy tree, capable of withstanding the harshest conditions.

5. Adaptability:
Adaptability should be regarded as a core strength. Like a river shaping its path through rugged landscapes, remain flexible and responsive on your journey.

6. Build a Support System:
Encircle yourself with a network of supportive, like-minded individuals. Their encouragement will bolster your motivation and focus.

7. Mindset:
Develop a mindset rooted in positivity and self-belief. This mindset will protect you from doubt and negativity, fostering a culture of perseverance.

8. Time Management:
Employ time management effectively. Each moment is a precious opportunity to advance toward your goals and craft your narrative of success.

9. Stay Informed:
Commit to lifelong learning. Diligently pursue knowledge and innovation to maintain a competitive edge in the dynamic entrepreneurial landscape.

10. Celebrate Successes:
Acknowledge and celebrate each success, irrespective of size. Each achievement is a testament to your dedication and hard work.

11. Financial Management:
Prioritize intelligent financial management as it is fundamental to achieving stability and growth. Incorporate it as a pivotal component of your entrepreneurial strategy.

12. Continuous Learning:
Embrace each challenge as a learning experience. Ongoing education is crucial to maintaining leadership and innovation in your industry.

Embrace the journey, for it is in the struggle that you find your strength, and in perseverance, you script your epic tale of triumph.

"To succeed, you have to accept failure as a path to growth. A person can choose to take that failure as their final point, OR use it to add fuel to the fire which ignites their passion to persist through. There are rare opportunities where a person achieves a goal on their first try, when in reality, it will take multiple attempts. Apply a goal as a drive to better yourself physically, mentally, intellectually and emotionally. Only you have the power to improve yourself, no one else can do that for you. You have to ask yourself the question, 'How can I be the best version of myself?'"

Kyle Schulze
The Deaf Ninja

The Deaf Ninja, 8+ years as an American Ninja Warrior contestant, first and only Deaf contestant to reach National Finals on the NBC TV Show. A Deaf competitor to face and compete through grueling stages of obstacle courses, overcome only by using his own strength, strategy, and dexterity. His success has granted his recognition among the top elite Ninjas across the world.

Now he keeps his passion alive through motivational speaking, with the hopes to inspire Deaf and Hard of Hearing adults and children to chase after their dreams and never give up!

> "The purpose of information is not knowledge.
>
> It is being able to take the right action."

Jim House
Subject Matter Expert on Accessible Emergency Communications

Jim House is the Disability Integration Manager for the Coalition on Inclusive Emergency Planning (CIEP) at the Washington State Independent Living Council. CIEP is a statewide advisory group that focuses on effective communications, programmatic and physical access, and other functional access needs (AFN) and issues impacting people with disabilities and other marginalized communities in emergencies. Under his leadership, CIEP has grown its stakeholder network to include community advocates with disabilities and AFN, emergency management professionals, and other community based organization leaders. CIEP stakeholders participate in planning, exercises, assessments, and other activities, leading to a growth in services in Washington such as Text-to-911, accessible alerting technologies, ASL Alerts, equitable public health responses, and more. Jim participated in several forums covering access issues with Information and Communications Technologies (ICT) before, during, and after disasters.

As a result of Jim's ongoing leadership and community involvement, Portland, Oregon passed the first captioning activation ordinance requiring all television sets in public places to display captions during business hours. This ordinance has been emulated in more than a dozen cities around the country.

As its former Board Member and Public Relations Director, Jim has supported Telecommunications for the Deaf and Hard of Hearing, Inc. (TDI) for many years. His accomplishments include a book, A PATH TOWARD AN ACCESSIBLE WORLD documenting TDI's 50 years of advocacy, implementing the Communications and Video Accessibility Act of 2010, numerous presentations on consumer advocacy, television and Internet captioning issues. He wrote successful grant proposals, some resulting in nearly $3M in federal funding to develop emergency preparedness training programs and other projects.

> "Enjoy the small moments. Don't get too caught up in the big picture and forget the little things – it is the little things that create momentum towards the big picture."

David Matchett-Putz
Real Estate Agent

David Matchett-Putz is an experienced real estate professional in Rochester, NY with expertise in the local market and a background in real estate investment.

Known for his trustworthiness and client-centric approach, David's success is built on strong support for his clients and keen market insight. David works with a variety of clients in the Western New York area, with a majority of his clients being deaf or hard of hearing.

David found his passion in real estate in 2019, when he moved back to Rochester, NY after living in Washington, D.C. for two years. He attended local real estate investment gatherings and events, and became interested in the business side of real estate and property management. David became a licensed realtor in 2022, and is dedicated to educating others about navigating real estate.

"Everybody has a story. Do not be afraid to tell yours and do not compare yours with others. Often times we see other people's success and it makes us feel more inferior to share ours. You do not have to fight bears just to get a great story just as much as you do not have to sit at your home, hoping someone will knock on your door to listen to your story. Share it. Say it. Be it. All you need to do is to continue on the path that you yearn to be on while listening to other people's stories. Everyone's timeline is different. Learn to celebrate others and then your time will come. Learn to congratulate others and then your time will come. Learn to cheer for others and then your time will come. Use people's stories as your inspiration, never as a comparison. Here's my own favorite saying – UPWARDS AND ONWARDS!"

Renca Dunn

Renca Dunn
Comedian and Advocate

Born in Hawaii but currently in Nebraska, Renca is not shy when it comes to moving around. She has moved over 30 times in her life ranging from living on a farm, in a busy city, and even on a commercial fishing boat at one time. Renca has lived in nine states and went to seven different schools: three Deaf schools and four mainstream schools. She graduated from Washington School for the Deaf and went off to Gallaudet University, achieving 3 BA degrees in English, Education, and Communication Studies. Renca continued her education journey by going to American University for her Master's in International Communication. A job opportunity in Iowa made Renca move from D.C. to Iowa and after her contract ended, she decided to go back to school for her doctoral studies. She is studying in the Interpersonal, Family, and Health field at the University of Nebraska Lincoln.

Besides her academic life, she comes from a 3rd generation of having a Deaf family and is on a journey to learn more about her Hispanic roots. Renca is a co-cheer coach at Iowa School for the Deaf, one of the reporters for The Daily Moth news, and is a content creator that makes entertaining videos on her social media platform known as ReallyRenca. She enjoys traveling, hiking, camping, and of course – drinking lattes. All of her life experiences have shaped her to be who she is today because of the people she met, the places she went, and the stories she learned about.

https://linktr.ee/reallyrenca

"You have too many flaws to be perfect, but you also have too many blessings to be ungrateful."

Warren Snipe
Hip Hop Recording Artist

Warren "WAWA" Snipe, a visionary Hip Hop Recording Artist from the D.C./MD/VA area, has been redefining the music landscape since 2005 with "Dip Hop" – Hip Hop through deaf eyes. His unique genre has not only garnered acclaim over the past 15+ years, but also educated the world about the capabilities of deaf musicians. WAWA's work, including his influential albums "Deaf: So What?!," "Unapologetically ____," and "Wamilton," exemplifies his understanding of turning dreams into reality by transforming perceived limitations into powerful artistic expressions.

Celebrated for his talent and determination, WAWA's performances at Super Bowl LV and LVI, and his appearances on shows like Black Lightning and Fear The Walking Dead, highlight his versatility and impact. WAWA continues to inspire, showing the world how vision, passion, and resilience can create profound change in the music and entertainment industry.

www.wawasworld.com

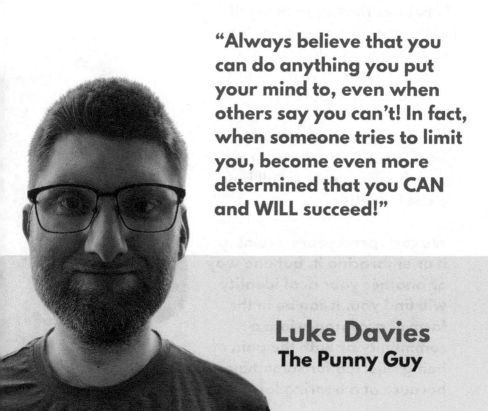

> **"Always believe that you can do anything you put your mind to, even when others say you can't! In fact, when someone tries to limit you, become even more determined that you CAN and WILL succeed!"**

Luke Davies
The Punny Guy

Luke considers himself lucky to have been born and raised in beautiful, lake-filled Minnesota where he still enjoys living today. Growing up, he had great support from family, friends, amazing educators, and DHH adults who believed in him, walking away from those who didn't.

Being someone who is Deaf Plus with specific health needs meant he needed to work harder and smarter. But the payoff has been that he now works full-time, lives on his own and is extremely independent. His funny, often "punny," positive attitude has served him well.

"I believe the key to living life with passion and success is to embrace yourself. It's not a straightforward journey but it's a beautiful journey.

No matter how we grew up as Deaf, deaf, hard of hearing, with hearing loss, we all have a deaf identity.

We can spend years avoiding it or embracing it, but one way or another your deaf identity will find you. It can be in the form of acceptance into a community or with the pain of being rejected for something because of a hearing loss.

I think the key is to embrace our deaf identities and learn about who we are. Dive into your community that accepts and understands you. That community is key. And the journey of embracing our identity is a beautiful path taken."

Janna Rovniak

Certified Peer Mentor

Janna Rovniak is a Certified Peer Mentor for the deaf and hard of hearing. She has been hard of hearing all her life and works with others through speaking, writing, workshops, and coaching to help overcome the stigma of hearing loss.

hardofhearingmama.com

"To be successful, you gotta hustle for something you're passionate about, grind through any obstacles that come your way, and weather the storm to get what you really want. That's the vibe of passion for success. Your advice is to never stop chasing your dreams, no matter what."

Harold Foxx

Writer, Producer, Actor, Comedian, Director

Harold Eugene Catron Jr., better known by his stage name Harold Foxx, is an aspiring screenwriter, comedian, director, producer, and actor who happens to be Deaf. Originally from Memphis, Tennessee, Harold graduated with a Bachelor's degree from Gallaudet University in Washington, D.C., where he played college football.

Best known for his stand-up comedy, Harold has performed at iconic venues such as the Crow Comedy, the Laugh Factory, Flappers Comedy Club, and the Palm Springs International Virtual Comedy Festival 2020, as well as in major cities nationwide.

Harold co-wrote, co-directed, and starred in **Open to Interpretation** for the 2024 Easterseals Disability Film Challenge, for which he was nominated as a Best Actor. He is also an Associate Producer for the documentary **Being Michelle** and was a post-production intern for a comedy-romantic feature film **Something from Tiffany's** by Amazon Studios.

Harold is also a graduate student at California State University, Northridge, pursuing an MFA (Master of Fine Arts) in Screenwriting.

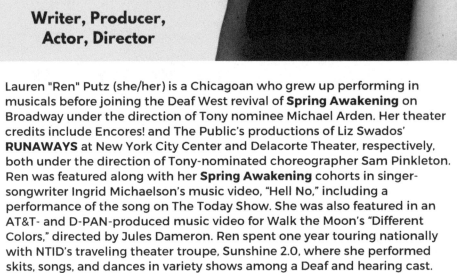

> "Do what makes you feel alive. Good energy begets more good energy."

Lauren "Ren" Putz

Writer, Producer, Actor, Director

Lauren "Ren" Putz (she/her) is a Chicagoan who grew up performing in musicals before joining the Deaf West revival of **Spring Awakening** on Broadway under the direction of Tony nominee Michael Arden. Her theater credits include Encores! and The Public's productions of Liz Swados' **RUNAWAYS** at New York City Center and Delacorte Theater, respectively, both under the direction of Tony-nominated choreographer Sam Pinkleton. Ren was featured along with her **Spring Awakening** cohorts in singer-songwriter Ingrid Michaelson's music video, "Hell No," including a performance of the song on The Today Show. She was also featured in an AT&T- and D-PAN-produced music video for Walk the Moon's "Different Colors," directed by Jules Dameron. Ren spent one year touring nationally with NTID's traveling theater troupe, Sunshine 2.0, where she performed skits, songs, and dances in variety shows among a Deaf and hearing cast.

Currently, Ren works as a director, producer, and editor at Morpheyes, a Deaf-led film studio in Rochester, NY. She is the co-director of their award-winning short film, **INSPIRED**, and the director of **Deaf And...**, a new docuseries exploring Deaf culture in America that features interviews with 18 Deaf scholars and creative professionals.

Additionally, Ren is a writer and editor whose work can be found in Sofia Seitchik's **The Light of Deaf Women** and B.B. Beaudreaux's **The Million Dollar Code**.

"My advice for a passionate and successful life includes continuous learning, resilience, embracing challenges, and fostering a supportive network. The intersection of my interests defines my unique perspective, driving innovation and a commitment to making a positive impact."

Adam Hsu
The Entrepreneur

I am in a Master of Science program in Technology, Innovation, Management, and Entrepreneurship at RIT. I graduated with a Bachelor of Applied Arts and Science degree in Chemistry and Entrepreneurship. I have always been a researcher. As a kid, I was always wondering how a business was set up, the logistics behind it, and how problems were to be solved. I also enjoyed reading **Rich Dad, Poor Dad**, and **Why We Want You to Be Rich** by Robert T. Kiyosaki. They became wealthy and handled money in a variety of ways, which inspired me.

I am a chemist because I enjoy analyzing and experimenting with many aspects of medicine, such as how it is designed to treat many people and how some are not effective. Recently, I had the opportunity to expand on my use of chemistry in dynamic permeability reduction and scaling of flow in porous media.

All of that is what inspired me to start my own company. I believe that many other Deaf people can establish their own ventures in their own way. I enjoy conducting background research and analyzing the topics involved, and I want to create a business for individuals who have a hard time finding a job because of disabilities and be their mentor.

I'm a chemist; I'm a researcher; but most importantly, I'm an entrepreneur. As an individual with experience in conducting scientific experiments, researching, and volunteering, I've worked various jobs at the Rochester Institute of Technology, providing a lot of community service to students and doing my best to help them. Currently, I am working with the Innovation Center at RIT to improve my knowledge of leadership, mentoring, and teaching people how to create a suitable business environment when developing ideas.

Scott Lehmann and Shayna Unger

Deaf Mountaineers, Explorers, Educators, and Storytellers

Scott Lehmann and Shayna Unger were both born into multigenerational deaf families and raised in the deaf community. Growing up, there wasn't much deaf representation in the outdoors and they faced limited access to outdoor education due to communication barriers. It wasn't after college that they both taught themselves to climb mountains by studying YouTube videos and asking other climbers on mountains using paper and pen to communicate.

Over the last ten years, Scott and Shayna have climbed the world's highest mountains like Kilimanjaro, Aconcagua, Denali, Mont Blanc and Matterhorn. Scott and Shayna were the first all-deaf team to summit Aconcagua and Denali. In May 2023, Shayna has become the first deaf woman in the world and Scott, the first deaf American to reach Mount Everest and Lhotse. These climbs made them the first deaf individuals to achieve a double ascent of 8000m back-to-back in just 26 hours. Their experience has inspired them to launch the "Seeing Beyond: Seven Summits" project with the aim of becoming the first deaf individuals to reach the Seven Summits, and to raise awareness, improve accessibility to information and education, increase deaf and disabled representation and inspire their community to explore outdoors.

www.scottshayna.com

"There is a spark of passion in you just waiting to be ignited. No matter how wild or big your life goals may seem to others, follow them, work for them, and never give up on them. Anything is possible if you dare to dream."

Scott Lehmann and Shayna Unger

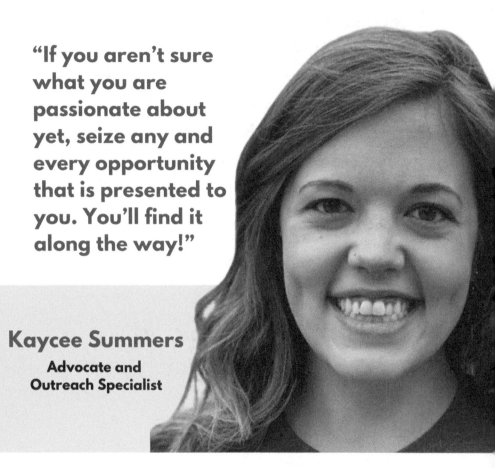

"If you aren't sure what you are passionate about yet, seize any and every opportunity that is presented to you. You'll find it along the way!"

Kaycee Summers

Advocate and Outreach Specialist

I hail from Colorado Springs and graduated from the Rochester Institute of Technology with my Bachelor of Science, and then my M.ED from Arizona State University.

As an Educator, Outreach Specialist, and advocate, I am passionate about working with D/HH individuals and present them with opportunities that allow them to explore the world, discover their identities as a D/HH individual and help them gain tools to navigate the world.

"The profound things are health, education, and gratitude. It's because, without health, you can't accomplish anything. Also, without education, you can't give physically, mentally, and socially to the world of work in life. Finally, without gratitude, you can't appreciate everything you are fortunate enough to occupy in life."

Deoraj Phatandain

Deafness is My Nature

My name is Deoraj Phatandain, and I'm from Guyana but raised in New York City.

I'm studying Civil Engineering Technology for my Bachelor of Science degree.

> "Never let one person stop you from achieving your dreams."

Kellina Powell
Deaf Queen Boss

Kellina is a deaf coach and advocate, a podcast speaker, a best-selling author, and a passionate entrepreneur on a mission to help young adults with disabilities achieve their goals while also educating others about the deaf community. What makes her story even more incredible is that Kellina is actually a hard of hearing person who lost 100% of her hearing at the young age of 4.

Being hard of hearing hasn't stopped her from pursuing her dreams including gaining her Bachelor's degree in Psychology from York University and post-graduate certificate in Mental Health and Addiction, becoming a life coach, and an Amazon best-selling author with her first book, "Everyday I Am Just Deaf."

Kellina encourages everyone in that no matter what your circumstances are, you can have everything you want in life. She continues to overcome the many challenges of living in a hearing world. Her message is clear: "Never let one person stop you from achieving your dreams."

"Live passionately; let your enthusiasm fuel your journey. Success follows when passion guides your path.

Stay resilient, learn from setbacks, and persist in your pursuits."

Abir Ameziane Hassani
Data Operator

In the face of hearing challenges, I've navigated life with resilience and determination. Overcoming obstacles, I've developed a unique perspective and honed valuable skills.

My journey is a testament to perseverance and a commitment to embracing opportunities despite any hurdles.

Michael E. Skyer
Deaf Education Researcher

Dr. Michael E. Skyer is a teacher educator who, for the past decade, has worked with deaf and nondeaf graduate students around the country and the world, who aspire to become future teachers of the deaf. Skyer's dissertation focused on grounded theories and case studies of visuality and multimodality in deaf pedagogies in higher education contexts. Prior to teacher education, Skyer taught writing at the undergraduate level for five years, and a mixture of public and residential (pK-12) deaf education settings, including the itinerant model, for three years. Skyer notes with amusement that he has taught the "LEGO age range," that is, his students are between the ages of 4 and 90, including pre-kindergarten children and inclusive of gerontological and community-based disability education. Skyer was recently featured in Scientific American for his insights into the digital contexts of deaf education concomitant with the COVID-19 pandemic.

"The praxis of passion is a synthesis of two things: doing what you love to do and doing what is feasible. Sometimes passions will wax and wane. Other times, your passion will act like a beacon and help you see what truly matters in your life. Your passion may be the antithesis of somebody else's passion, and that is okay.

Early in my life, I was actively discouraged from following what I loved to do, but eventually I found a way to do it. I had to work very hard to get to the point where my passion is what I earn a living doing. If you use your passion like a compass, it can help you decide what to focus on and what not to focus on.

Here is an axiom that needs to be unpacked: "Do what you love and you will never work a day in your life." This axiom is not true, but it does contain seeds of truth. Passions require work. Work is needed to nurture, to develop, and to exercise the skills that underlie your passion. When those processes are enjoyed, the work seems to disappear – but the work itself does not disappear. Be mindful that success occurs because you have dedicated yourself to working your passion. That requires theory, action, and reflection (praxis) all at once. This happens precisely by working the juncture between what you love and what you can do pragmatically."

Michael E. Skyer

Melissa Elmira Yingst

MELMIRA

Melissa Elmira Yingst is a dedicated professional with a passion for unearthing hidden narratives and promoting social awareness, particularly feminist causes. Her commitment to fostering deep connections with others has since grown into a career marked by a profound dedication to community engagement.

After earning her Bachelor's degree in Psychology from Gallaudet University and her Master's degree in Social Work from Arizona State University, Melissa held a variety of roles in the social work and counseling fields. She has worked as a social worker and school counselor in both NYC and Phoenix, and currently serves as EVP of Outreach & Partnerships with VSYN+ while teaching at CSUN.

In addition to her professional pursuits, Melissa is a passionate advocate for social justice and community empowerment. She is actively involved with Council de Manos, an organization dedicated to ending injustice within the Deaf Latinx community, as well as Signed by Stories, a mental health advocacy group. Her dedication to these causes is a reflection of her strong commitment to creating positive change in the world.

Melissa's passion for media is also evident in her work on her acclaimed show, MELMIRA, where she fosters open and honest conversations around important social issues. Melissa is known for her signature red lipstick, which she wears as a symbol of her strength and commitment to making a difference. She is a dynamic force in the field of social work and counseling, and her unwavering dedication to being real is an inspiration to all who know her.

www.melissayingst.com

106

Melissa Elmira Yingst

"Embrace a profound love for life as the driving force behind your pursuit of passion and success. Infuse every endeavor with genuine heart and dedication, recognizing that a deep passion requires sincere commitment.

Embracing vulnerability as a strength, allow yourself to take risks and learn from setbacks on the path to success.

Lastly, maintain a sense of humor, as laughter not only lightens the journey but also serves as a powerful tool for resilience in the face of challenges."

"Spend time in nature: Nature holds a powerful mirror to the soul, helping us reconnect with our authentic selves.

Practice mindfulness: Be present in the moment, noticing what truly brings you joy and excitement.

Embrace imperfection: Perfectionism stifles passion. Celebrate your unique quirks and flaws."

Nature and Forest Therapy Guide

Summer Crider

Summer Crider, a passionate Deaf Nature and Forest Therapy guide, leads transformative journeys through forest bathing. Previously an ASL and Deaf Studies professor and filmmaker, they traded the traditional classrooms for forests, immersing themself in nature connection and gently guiding others to find their place in the world.

"The Giving Cypress," their guiding company, challenges limitations. Beyond language and societal norms, Summer helps us tap into the silent wisdom within, offering solo sessions and retreats focused on self-discovery and healing. Through walks, trails, and even foraging for "plant magic," they unlock the profound healing secrets whispered by the forest.

> "I know that so many deaf/hard of hearing individuals struggle with navigating the hearing world. I would like to encourage these individuals to embrace their disability and use it to enable themselves; don't just look at it as a burden but more of an opportunity to uniquely get to know yourself and strengths in this walk of life."

Miriam Durodola
Artist, Adventurous, Ace

Miriam Durodola is currently a sophomore at Georgia State University, pursuing a degree in Business with a major in Computer Information Systems and a focus on Data Analytics. Miriam was born in Jos, Nigeria, and has two brothers, in a family of five. Miriam lost her hearing at the young age of seven, moved to New York to have her cochlear implant surgery, and later moved down to Georgia. Miriam attended Beaulah Elementary School and later graduated with honors from Villa Rica High School, where she was recognized as a Carroll County Scholar. During her time at Villa Rica High School, Miriam was involved in various extracurricular activities, including the Air Force Reserve Officer Training Corps (ROTC), Yearbook, Student Government Association, Purple Pearls, Drill Team, and Kitty Hawk Honor Society, showcasing her commitment to leadership and discipline, despite her deafness.

Currently a sophomore at Georgia State University, Miriam is a member of Women in Technology, College Girls Rock, SOUL, and the Tennis Club. She plans to further her learning in the Computer Science field and hopes to secure an internship at Microsoft, expressing her dedication to academic and professional development. Miriam is passionate about learning new skills and is currently exploring design. She aspires to establish a presence in the interior design industry as a personal interest. Looking ahead, Miriam envisions contributing to her community by volunteering with the United Nations (UN). Post-graduation, she plans to work in a field related to Data Analytics, aligning with her academic focus.

"Live passionately; let your enthusiasm fuel your journey. Success follows when passion guides your path.

Stay resilient, learn from setbacks, and persist in your pursuits."

Dr. Jasmine Simmons

Audiologist, Author, and Accessibility Consultant

Dr. Simmons' educational path began at the University of Akron, where she obtained her undergraduate degree. Her determination for knowledge and passion for audiology led her to Central Michigan University, where she earned her Doctorate in Audiology, solidifying her expertise in the field.

Born profoundly deaf, she received a cochlear implant at the age of two. It provided her with a remarkable perspective on the world of audiology. She also faces the challenges of Usher's syndrome, which has caused progressive vision loss due to retinitis pigmentosa.

Dr. Simmons firmly believes that every child should be able to see themselves in the pages of books, and she's actively working on her first children's book series, aimed at promoting awareness, acceptance, and inclusion. Her dedication to creating a more inclusive world extends to her public speaking engagements, where she passionately advocates for better healthcare and job opportunities for people with disabilities.

Currently, Dr. Simmons is a purposeful audiologist at the nonprofit Jacksonville Speech and Hearing Clinic. Dr. Jasmine Simmons is not just an audiologist; she is a lantern of hope, a role model, and a driving force behind a more inclusive and accepting world for everyone.

www.DrJasmineSimmons.com & www.instagram.com/DrJasmineSimmons

> "Don't let others tell you that you can't do anything because of your hearing loss. You are capable of anything!"

Rosanna Napolitano

Audiology Student

Rosanna Napolitano has been a bilateral cochlear implant user for more than 10 years now. She proudly holds a Bachelor's degree in Speech and Communication Disorders from Nova Southeastern University and is actively engaged as an audiologist assistant as she pursues her doctoral studies in Audiology. Moreover, Rosanna is proficient in both Spanish and English, enabling her to effectively communicate in a bilingual capacity.

As a future audiologist with cochlear implants, she is driven to exemplify that hearing loss should not limit one's professional aspirations or ability to support others with similar challenges. Her personal journey as a deaf individual serves as the inspiration for her pursuit of this career, igniting a passion to overcome barriers and make a meaningful difference in the lives of those affected by hearing loss.

www.instagram.com/YoSoyRobotina

"I hope this can inspire others and be a reminder of the importance of fostering inclusive environments:

With effort and self-belief we can achieve our dreams regardless of obstacles we face."

Laura Alicia
The Latin Photographer

My name is Laura Alicia and I was born with profound bilateral hearing loss. Growing up in a hearing environment, I had no access to learning sign language. I tried to learn ASL, Auslan, and LSM, but they require extensive ongoing practice. I wore hearing aids from early childhood until age 18, when I got a cochlear implant surgery which was life-changing. The implant greatly improved my self-confidence and ability to understand others and make myself understood. I even learned two additional languages, English and Italian.

I currently live in Melbourne, Australia and run my own business as a freelance commercial photographer. It was challenging to get here, but my passion for photography and perseverance have helped me excel. I still face barriers due to my disability, but I continually seek to connect with both the hearing community and the Deaf community. My biggest motivation is showing that with support and a positive attitude, a disability does not define your limits.

"You are more than your disability. Go toward things that define you."

Anthony Imafidon

"Deaf Go-Getter"
Entrepreneur,
Motivational Speaker,
Disability Advocate

Anthony Imafidon was born and raised in Queens, New York. He faced many challenges growing up, including being placed in special education and struggling with reading and writing. But Anthony didn't let these obstacles stop him.

Inspired by role models who overcame their own difficulties, Anthony decided to work hard and achieve his dreams. He believed that with determination and perseverance, anything is possible.

Today, Anthony Imafidon is a respected motivational speaker and successful entrepreneur. Through his speeches and business ventures, he inspires the next generation to reach their full potential. Anthony's story shows that with hard work, anyone can overcome challenges and achieve their dreams.

www.instagram.com/DeafGoGetter

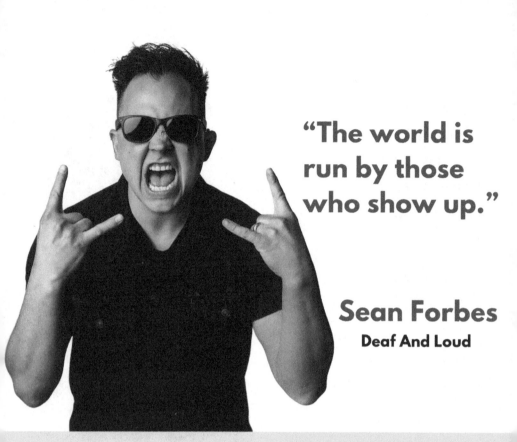

"The world is run by those who show up."

Sean Forbes
Deaf And Loud

Sean Forbes is an award-winning musician and songwriter from Detroit. Born into a musical family, Sean received a drum set when he was five years old and never stopped playing. Realizing that he was different from a young age, Sean never gave up on pursuing his passion for music despite his deafness. While attending NTID/RIT, he realized that his calling was to work on making music accessible for the deaf and hard of hearing community. He returned to Detroit to form D-PAN, the Deaf Professional Arts Network, a nonprofit focused on access in media and entertainment. In 2010 he signed a record deal with Eminem's production team and released his first song "I'm Deaf," made an album called "Perfect Imperfection," and travelled the world performing. In 2020 he released his sophomore album "Little Victories" and was the #1 Rap artist on many music charts. In 2022, he performed at Super Bowl LVI alongside Warren "Wawa" Snipe for his favorite rap artists Dr. Dre, Snoop Dogg, Eminem, and more.

www.deafandloud.com and www.dpan.tv

"Try everything. I started to try to make a habit to not say no to any request or offer to try a new project that may have been outside my realm of experience, skill set, or comfort zone. That's how I have come to grow, and so may opportunities have opened up to me. I've discovered that I can excel at, and even enjoy, certain fields that I didn't think would be any interest to me. This has allowed me to be able to choose my career path, and although it is a little cliche, I do truly believe in doing what I love. My work never feels like work, and I can keep on building experience and skills to share with future generations of Deaf and Hard of Hearing individuals."

I grew up mainstreamed in California, but didn't really use ASL or get involved with the Deaf community until I went to college. This is when I realized I could express myself in a language that gave me complete freedom. Since college, I have worked as an actor, theatre interpreter, DASL, director, performer, workshop presenter, writer, translator, summer camp director, artist in residence, social events coordinator, and college professor. I currently teach at a private college in Chicago, but continue to travel for presentations and performances when not working on my personal projects, reading, and spending time with my family.

Crom Saunders
Lifelong Learner

"Always believe in yourself and never give up, the sky is the limit."

Kai Petersen
Car Painter

I'm a hard of hearing and autistic National 1st-place winner in car painting, who has a true passion for painting cars. I've always received loads of guidance and support throughout learning this trade for the past three years. I will be participating in the World Skills Lyon competition September 2024 for car painting against people from all over the world. I've always enjoyed being around cars, so for me it's no shocker that I chose a career path that has to do with working on cars...

Because of my young age of 16, I think I inspire lots of younger people to push to get their dreams, and that you don't need to be a certain age to start getting your goals or to even make goals.

"Authenticity serves as the foundation for a life filled with passion and success. When you are true to yourself, your passions naturally align with your actions and decisions, and you just can't help but naturally live a more fulfilling and purpose-driven life."

Rachel Burton
Such a Lovely Red

Rachel Burton, affectionately known as Rach, stands as a resilient force, weaving her captivating narrative on Such A Lovely Red.

In her professional realm, Rach serves as the Director of Strategy and Initiatives at dozanū, a dynamic full-service marketing company. As an early digital native who grew up with a keyboard always at her fingertips, Rach remains fascinated by the power of a single message to transcend diverse channels. A proud alumna of Gallaudet University, she earned her BA in Sociology. Her neurodiverse perspective is a badge of honor, and her bilingual upbringing, coupled with a lifelong background in communications, led her to a Master's degree in Media, Culture, and Communication from New York University.

Beyond her professional pursuits, Rach is deeply immersed in contributing to her community, particularly as a deaf woman. Currently serving as the Vice Chair on the Board of Deaf Women United, and as a team member for Deaf Artisan Market Day, she dedicates her time to several other organizations. In these roles, she offers invaluable insights and unwavering support, contributing significantly to the empowerment and visibility of the deaf community. Her contributions extend beyond boardrooms and committees, as she is a constant presence in community organizations, volunteering her time with enthusiasm.

suchalovelyred.com 117

Rachel Soudakoff and Rachel Berry
The Deaf Adventurers

Rachel Soudakoff and Rachel Berry are a dynamic married couple who turned their passion for travel and event organization into a thriving business. In 2021, they founded Deaf Adventures in New Zealand, a company dedicated to providing accessible tours led by Deaf guides for Deaf travelers worldwide.

As avid travelers, Rachel and Rachel noticed a significant gap in the travel industry regarding accessibility for Deaf individuals. This inspired them to create Deaf Adventures, aiming to offer inclusive and immersive travel experiences. Since its establishment, the company has welcomed over 100 adventurers from various corners of the globe, operating tours in more than 10 destinations, including New Zealand, the United States, and several countries across Europe.

www.deafadventures.nz

"Our advice is to follow your heart and pursue what genuinely excites you. Embrace your passions and don't be afraid to turn them into your life's work.

Success comes when you combine your love for what you do with dedication and hard work. Surround yourself with supportive people who share your vision and values. Always be open to learning and growing, and never lose sight of the impact you want to make.

For us, turning our passion for travel and inclusivity into Deaf Adventures has been a journey of both challenges and incredible rewards.

Remember, true success is not just about achieving your goals, but also about enjoying the journey and making a positive difference along the way."

Rachel Soudakoff
and Rachel Berry

"Living your life with Passion and Success is being willing to accept that things will scare you and you will doubt yourself a lot. It's ok to admit that you are nervous or afraid or that something is new and you don't have the road map. Just don't let any of that stop you. If you strive for perfection in everything you do, then you will not enjoy the journey. Allow yourself to have a beginner's mind, even about things you have mastered. This kind of attitude will take the pressure off of making mistakes. Because, while no one enjoys making mistakes, they are the catalyst for real growth."

Matt Daigle
Artist, Humorist, Writer, and Educator

Matt Daigle is a comedic writer, award-winning illustrator, designer and the cartoonist/co-creator of the webcomic That Deaf Guy. Matt has published two humor books, Extreme Interpreting and In Deaf Culture. With his wife Kay, he has published two books, That Deaf Guy: A Family Portrait and That Deaf Guy: A Wild Ride. Matt is also the co-creator and co-writer for "Harmonium," a new video game currently in development. In addition to his creative work, Matt holds a Master's degree from Gallaudet University in Sign Language Education and is a professor at California State University Northridge in the Deaf Studies Department.

A self-professed coffee addict, Matt loves to read poetry, binge on tv shows, and spend time with his family trying new cuisine around Los Angeles.

www.handsail.net

"Your passion is part of your test. Remember to chase your passion relentlessly; it's the heartbeat of your purpose and then you will see the light of success."

Nakia Smith

Activist and Social Media Influencer

Texas-raised, mid 20s, engaged and have one lovely son. I'm well-known for spreading BASL (Black American Sign Language) on social media in late 2020 during COVID.

www.instagram.com/itscharmay

"Former President Theodore Roosevelt once said that 'Comparison is the thief of joy.' I believe this to be wholeheartedly true. There will never be anyone else exactly like you in this world. Forge your own way in life. Do the things that you love. Take that vacation. Buy that dress. Do what sparks joy. In the end, those are the things that you will remember the most."

Aileen Pagán-Welch

Rehabilitation Counselor for the Deaf

Aileen Pagán-Welch was born and raised in the Bronx, New York City. She was raised bilingual, speaking Spanish and English, before being diagnosed as Deaf as a child. She quickly adapted and learned American Sign Language. Aileen graduated from the Rochester Institute of Technology, having earned both a Bachelor's and Master's degree while enrolled.

In 2020, after settling into the Columbia area with her family, she began working with the SC Vocational Rehabilitation Department. Aileen serves as the Regional Rehabilitation Counselor for the Deaf and works with Deaf adults and Deaf transition students in the Midlands area of SC. She provides rehabilitation counseling services, assists with obtaining and maintaining employment, provides access to training and evaluation, provides services such as ASL interpreters for classes or job interviews, counsels about post-secondary education options, teaches self-advocacy skills and much, much more. Being trilingual, the ability to use direct communication with clients, as well as personal experience and identity with Deaf culture, has allowed her to support clients in obtaining educational and career opportunities.

A leader in the Deaf community, she also serves as a Board member for both the SC Association for the Deaf (SCAD) and Beginnings, SC, with the intent of creating positive change for the Deaf community. An avid student, Aileen is continuing her education and is in her second year at the USC Rehabilitation Counseling program. Married to her college sweetheart since 1997... Aileen is a proud and loving mother of three amazing kiddos.

> **"Allow yourself to be curious. Curiosity takes you places that you never thought you would go. Be open to life."**

Joseph C. Hill
Professor of Curiosity

Joseph C. Hill is a black deaf university professor of linguistics who is interested in everything that stimulates his mind. As the youngest of his deaf and hard of hearing siblings by at least 11 years, he saw the possibility for himself by watching his older sister and brothers going off to college. The possibility excited him because he loved school. Education was an escape for him, figuratively and literally, because life was too limiting and lonely for him as a deaf child. When he finally went to college, he realized there's more to life than grades and awards. He became curious and followed through with his choices that put him on the path to higher education. He earned his BS degree in Systems Analysis at Miami University of Ohio and his MA and Ph.D degrees in Linguistics at Gallaudet University. He became an assistant professor at the University of North Carolina at Greensboro and an associate professor at the Rochester Institute of Technology. Now he's a center director of Black Deaf Studies at Gallaudet University with the title of Full Professor. He's also a multilingual polymath, a world traveler, a Lindy Hop dancer, a tarot card reader, a Reiki practitioner, a boat operator, and whatever he can be. Life is his education

www.josephchill.com

"Success is personal and varies for everyone. It's not just about money or fame but about finding and pursuing your passion. Living with passion means engaging in what excites and fulfills you, bringing joy and purpose to your life.

Success is the satisfaction of living authentically and doing what you love. It's about setting goals, overcoming challenges, and growing.

Listen to your inner voice, discover what drives you, and pursue it relentlessly. Embrace your unique path, celebrate your progress, and enjoy the journey. True success lies in how deeply you live and love each moment."

Nikki Reineck

Nikki Reineck

CEO of Sisters in Style

Nikki Reineck, a visionary entrepreneur, is the proud owner of Sisters in Style, a thriving e-commerce venture. With four successful years in operation, Nikki's commitment to excellence has elevated Sisters in Style to new heights.

Notably, Nikki's dedication to inclusivity is a hallmark of her business. After selling the storefront to a new deaf owner in Frederick, MD, Nikki fostered a unique environment where deaf employees play a pivotal role. This distinctive approach has forged strong connections between customers and the boutique, setting Sisters in Style apart in the world of fashion. American Sign Language (ASL) is seamlessly integrated across all platforms, reflecting her belief in creating an accessible and welcoming space for everyone. Also, she creates countless job opportunities for deaf women and donates money to deaf nonprofit organizations.

Beyond her entrepreneurial pursuits, Nikki finds joy in her family life. Married to Michael, she is a proud mother to two wonderful children, Arianna and Brett. In her leisure time, Nikki indulges her passion for business literature, immersing herself in insightful reads. She also stays informed and inspired through podcasts while actively seeking opportunities to connect with new people.

Nikki Reineck's journey is not just about fashion; it's about creating a community, breaking barriers, and embracing diversity in the world of style.

www.sistersinstyleonline.com

"We may have a hearing loss, but our hearing loss does not have us, own us, or control us. Don't let your hearing loss define you... let it refine you, purge you, mold you, empower you and propel you forward. I've always believed that REFINEMENT is greater than DEFINEMENT! It forces you to learn the lessons of PERSEVERANCE, HARD WORK, and SUCCESS! But, most importantly, it teaches you exactly WHO YOU ARE and what YOU ARE CAPABLE OF!

Don't Limit Your Challenges... CHALLENGE YOUR LIMITS!"

Justin Osmond

Speaker, Author, Producer, Humanitarian

Justin knows firsthand what it is like to live in a world without sound. In his recently published book "Hearing with my Heart," he shares his story with the world in order to help all people understand the struggles of having a hearing loss and how to overcome them. He lives every day by his personal motto: "I may have a hearing loss, but that hearing loss does not have me."

www.justinosmond.com

> "Pay attention to your self-talk. What you tell yourself everyday becomes true. It can fuel your growth or lead to your downfall. Your words and actions are the keys to your destiny."

Melissa "echo" Greenlee
Deaf Entrepreneur

At the age of eight, Melissa "echo" Greenlee faced a life-changing event: the loss of her hearing. This pivotal moment set her on a path of self-advocacy.

In 2012, she founded deaffriendly.com, a review platform that empowers Deaf and hard of hearing people to share their experiences in a place of business. Echo's vision extends to creating a deaf-friendly world for 433 million Deaf and hard of hearing individuals around the globe. Through deaffriendly CONSULTING, launched in 2016, she collaborates with a diverse range of businesses, from small mom and pop businesses to Fortune 500 giants, guiding them towards practices that foster inclusivity and understanding.

www.deaffriendly.com

"Don't let anyone tell you that you can't succeed or achieve something because you can't hear. Don't let that stop you from doing what you want to do in your life. You will always figure out how to get things done, and you will realize that all your hard work and effort have paid off because people like us don't give up. We're resilient and can adapt to adverse situations. Let's turn our detractors into cheerleaders. And don't forget to be your own motivation! I know that you have worked twice as hard as everyone else to get ahead, but someday maybe people will start to look at you as an incredible person beyond your disability and how far you've come."

Yasiris Gomez

Yasiris Gomez

**Product Designer,
CEO of Deaf Pwr**

Yasiris Gomez is a Deaf Dominican passionate accessibility advocate and multidisciplinary designer. She has a degree in Industrial Design from INTEC, where her curiosity for solving real-world problems and unmet needs, particularly for marginalized groups, took root. During this journey, she discovered a significant gap in accessibility products for people with disabilities, a concern often overlooked in the early stages of design. This discovery motivated her to pursue a career in Interaction Design with a minor in High-Tech Entrepreneurship at Harbour.Space University.

Her belief that design and technology can improve people's lives drives her commitment to creating accessible solutions. This focus led her to develop innovative solutions for the Deaf community, earning her recognition as a 1st- and 2nd-place winner in hackathons organized by Microsoft Azure Latin America 2022 and OGTIC Dominican Republic. She was also honored with an honorable mention at Startup Weekend Santo Domingo 2022 and secured 1st place in the INTEC Emprende Business Ideas Pre-incubation Program 2023.

Growing up in a hearing environment presented its challenges, but Yasiris turned to education as her refuge. It was not only a source of knowledge, but also a space where she could overcome doubts and skepticism from hearing teachers who failed to recognize her full potential. Education became the foundation upon which she built her resilience and determination to prove her capabilities. In addition to her academic and professional achievements, Yasiris is the Founder and CEO of Deaf Pwr, a platform dedicated to raising awareness about the Deaf community in the Dominican Republic.

yasirisgomez.medium.com

129

> "True servant leadership is not just about achieving ambitious goals; it's about empowering others to share in the strong desire for a collaborative future. Every decision made reflects not only the world we live in today but shapes the world we leave for our children tomorrow."

Wendy Adams

Vice President,
Policy and Advocacy

Wendy Adams has charted a dynamic career within Sorenson, showcasing exceptional leadership and a deep commitment to fostering an inclusive workplace culture. Her passion for championing diversity, equity, inclusion, and accessibility is evident in both her professional journey and her active role within the organization.

As a Deaf woman, Wendy enthusiastically participates in projects focused on accessibility, dedicating her expertise to various initiatives. Her impactful contributions extend beyond the corporate sphere, as she volunteers with multiple organizations, leveraging her skills to make a positive impact. Wendy's dedication to these values underscores her role as a proactive advocate for a more diverse and accessible community.

"Once you set your goals – never give up until you reach them. The key is patience, persistence, and faith in reaching your dream. No one can take your dream away."

Jasmin Simpson

**Mental Health
Counselor**

I am from Ontario, Canada. I am deafblind. I was born in South Korea, and I was adopted when I was 16 months old. I experienced some language deprivation and I learned literacy and fingerspelling A to Z / ASL when I was six years old, but I knew my name and basic sign language / gestures before age six. I graduated with a Bachelor's in Social Work and a Master's in Social Work from Gallaudet University. I have been working as a mental health counselor for 15 years, including social work while I was a student – for a total of over 20 years of experience. When there is injustice, I fight to make things better. For example: I fought and won my case against both federal and provincial governments to make the student loan debt load more fair for students with disabilities. It took 18 years, but perseverance was key to my winning. This case helped many disabled students in Canada.

"To do anything big, get help. Convince others they want to do what you want to do. Be humble. Work hard. Never give up!"

Vint Cerf
Google's Chief Internet Evangelist

Vint Cerf
Google's Chief Internet Evangelist

Vinton G. Cerf has served as Vice President and Chief Internet Evangelist for Google since October 2005. In this role, he contributes to global policy development and continued standardization and spread of the Internet. He is also an active public face for Google in the Internet world.

Widely known as one of the "Fathers of the Internet," Cerf is the co-designer of the TCP/IP protocols and the architecture of the Internet. In December 1997, President Clinton presented the U.S. National Medal of Technology to Cerf and his colleague, Robert E. Kahn, for founding and developing the Internet. Kahn and Cerf were named the recipients of the ACM Alan M. Turing award in 2004 for their work on the Internet protocols. The ACM Turing award is sometimes called the "Nobel Prize of Computer Science." In November 2005, President George Bush awarded Cerf and Kahn the Presidential Medal of Freedom for their work. The medal is the highest civilian award given by the United States to its citizens. In April 2008, Cerf and Kahn received the prestigious Japan Prize and in 2013 Cerf, Kahn and three others received the Queen Elizabeth Prize in Engineering. Cerf was made an officer of the French Legion d'Honneur in December 2014 and Foreign Member of the British Royal Society in July 2016. In 2018 together with Robert Kahn, he received the Franklin Medal. In 2023, Cerf was awarded the IEEE Medal of Honor and the Marconi Society Lifetime Achievement Award.

Prior to rejoining MCI in 1994, Cerf was vice president of the Corporation for National Research Initiatives (CNRI) where he worked on information infrastructure and digital libraries. As vice president of MCI Digital Information Services from 1982-1986, he led the engineering of MCI Mail, the first commercial email service to be connected to the Internet. During his tenure from 1976-1982 with the U.S. Department of Defense's Advanced Research Projects Agency (DARPA), Cerf played a key role leading the development of Internet and Internet-related packet data transport and security technologies.

He serves as an advisor to many US Government agencies, including the National Science Foundation, the National Aeronautics and Space Administration, the US Departments of Defense, and Energy and Commerce.

> **"Stay conscious of how the food you consume affects your body, and navigate through the conflicting realms of established science and evolving knowledge with an open mind."**

A Health-Conscious Connoisseur

Samantha Wilson

Samantha Wilson, born deaf to deaf parents, spent her formative years in a residential school for the deaf, where the school meals often left much to be desired. This early exposure instilled in her a profound appreciation for wholesome, nourishing food. Weekends spent at her country home with a garden became cherished moments for indulging in real food before returning to school each week. Samantha's innate discernment for quality sustenance was evident from a young age, as she keenly felt the adverse effects of poor dietary choices. As she matured, Samantha encountered a pivotal moment when her beloved partner fell seriously ill, prompting an exhaustive search for answers. Through the guidance of a naturopath, they uncovered the root cause, igniting Samantha's passion for holistic health. Samantha is recognized as a holistic individual adept at identifying harmful chemicals and ingredients present in food and everyday products. You can find her easy, healthy recipes on her Instagram and Facebook: @samalouisaa.

> **"You will always face obstacles – learn to see them as your best friend, no matter how hard they are. Believe in yourself and that you can overcome them."**

Samara Maldonado
Student and Staff at RIT

I am a Deaf Latina first-generation college student and a student pursuing a Master's degree. I have faced many different obstacles in different ways. My high school teacher told me that I will not succeed in college as a Deaf person because I was not good at English writing. That was my first obstacle and I will never forget what the teacher said – it changed who I am today. It's not about proving the teachers, families, or others wrong. It's about believing in yourself.

The quote above reframes obstacles as valuable companions in life rather than enemies. In addition, embrace challenges as opportunities for improvement and see them as a natural part of personal and professional development. The key message is to have confidence in yourself and your capacity to overcome challenges, no matter how tough they are.

"My advice would be to always challenge yourself and most importantly, remember that you are the author of your destiny. Self-love and self-care promote Perseverance, Dedication, and Faith. Embrace and nurture your uniqueness."

Danielle Claxton

Philosopher of Positivity

I am Hard of Hearing and a graduate student working on my Master's degree in Clinical Mental Health Counseling.

I have two beautiful daughters who are also Hard of Hearing. I have over ten years of experience working in the Deaf/Hard of Hearing community.

> "Keep pushing forward with your ideas, ambitions, and goals. One day, dreams will become reality because of hard work that you have done and then, only then you can enjoy the delicious fruit of your labors."

Matthew Cummings
The Trapped Poet

I'm Deaf Disabled with Cerebral Palsy. I write poetry. It's my passion. I graduated from Rock Valley College after bouncing around colleges for 12 years. I'm planning on going back to Rock Valley College for their Mass Communication certification program, then transferring to Northern Illinois University in Dekalb. One of my biggest goals is to live independently in my apartment with a part-time aide. I'm certainly bigger than life –because life is short, so I want to make the best of it while I still can.

www.trappedpoet.wordpress.com

> "You are not in the same race as everyone else. Learn to appreciate forward movement, no matter how slow it is.
>
> You are a miracle.
>
> What are you waiting for? Get in the game!"

Melissa Skyer

Mosaic Artist and Environmental Scientist

Melissa became deaf in her twenties. Brilliant mosaic artist, scholar, author of two books, and an environmental scientist. She obtained a BA in Biology and an MA in Environmental Science from RIT. She worked for an engineering firm in Chicago, and in Southern California a gas company in Los Angeles. She taught science at the Rochester Institute of Technology. Melissa was passionate about education and preserving the environment.

Melissa also undertook Project Lead the Way efforts at Gananda High School, where she delivered presentations in the area of biomedical science and specifically on various issues related to deafness. She was an active supporter of NTID Outreach activities, including health science careers and agriculture camps for deaf and hard of hearing high school students in California. Locally, Melissa joined the nonprofit Genesee River Watch in 2019 as a member of the Board of Directors, where she participated on the technical and educational sub-committees of this group.

Melissa passed away shortly after her 40th birthday from a brain tumor.

"In my mind, life is about growing, contributing, being part of a community, and then working with that community to provide new opportunities for growth, like learning new skills to carry with us for the rest of our lives and teach others. I am considered disabled not because I am Deaf, but because of a society that treats Deaf individuals as unequal to hearing individuals. The world may try to teach us that we can't, but I believe we are all born to do what can't be done. This reminds me of a quote by St. Francis of Assisi, which has guided me through my entire life: 'Start by doing what's necessary; then do what's possible; and suddenly you are doing the impossible.'"

Dr. Amie Fornah-Sankoh

Deaf Scientist

Amie Fornah-Sankoh got her Ph.D from the University of Tennessee's Department of Biochemistry & Cellular and Molecular Biology. Her scientific journey began at the Rochester Institute of Technology and National Technical Institute for the Deaf (RIT/NTID), where she earned Laboratory Science Technology and Biochemistry degrees before joining the University of Tennessee for her Ph.D.

In 2023, Amie made history as the first Deaf Black woman to earn a STEM doctorate. This milestone reflects her journey of perseverance and achievement, reaching its culminating point in her selection as the featured speaker for her university's 2023 Graduate Hooding Ceremony. Her most fulfilling realization is that she can excel as a scientist and a community advocate.

Currently, Amie serves as a Senior Research Specialist at Dow Coating Materials, where she contributes to the development of innovative waterborne barrier coatings for paper, enhancing functional performance and promoting recyclability in paper-based packaging applications.

www.instagram.com/deaf_scientist

"Don't let someone limit your dreams. Don't let someone else tell you what you can and can't do.

Only you know what you're capable of and honestly, you won't know what that is until you try. I encourage you to try out for that sport team or role in a play. I encourage you to take a hard class that everyone else thinks you'll fail or you won't like.

I spent too much time hiding who I was created to be. It wasn't until I threw off the shackles others gave me that I began to live a passionate, successful life. I wouldn't have become The Sassy Baker, a high school teacher, a published author, or a business owner if I had believed the lies of, 'You're not good enough.' You are enough just the way you are.

Go after your dreams. You might surprise yourself how far you can go."

Ruth Jackson

Ruth Jackson
The Sassy Baker

I grew up in Connecticut with a hearing family who didn't know ASL. At age five, I got hearing aids and started speech therapy, which lasted until middle school. Growing up, I was an avid reader because it was an escape into a world I chose rather than dealing with the struggle of communicating. My ASL learning journey started in 8th grade when I discovered the ASL alphabet in the back of my dictionary. Then I enrolled in ASL classes at the American School for the Deaf. For the next 10 years, I dove into this new world. I didn't know a space where I could thrive existed!

Fast forward to 2020 during the lockdown, I created a YouTube channel called The Sassy Baker where I made some family favorite recipes in ASL. Shortly after, I started dreaming about how I could be the role model I never had. How could I be a good resource for parents and D/deaf kids? God provided me with an answer – a community center. This way kids of all ages, regardless if they go to a Deaf school or not, will be able to meet others just like them. Bake it with Sass, my online business, was born to not only fuse my two passions – baking and ASL – but also provide connections and funding for my big dream.

I grew up feeling alone and ignored by my peers and my family. I don't want that for any other Deaf child. Some people don't realize how hard the hearing world makes it to be Deaf. Being Deaf isn't the issue, it's how we are treated that we have to fight. If we were all concerned about each other's needs, I think the Deaf community wouldn't have to fight so hard.

www.bakeitwithsass.com

"If you haven't found your passion, seek it. You cannot be successful until you know what you want. Once you have found your passion, build your path to success. To build your path to success, you must know who you are and what you want to do to get to where you are."

Gunner Woodall-Ryan

The Role Model

Gunner Woodall-Ryan is the first Deaf individual in his family. He was raised in the hearing world without knowledge of the Deaf community until his time at Gallaudet University, when he started college at 19 years old. This 2014 discovery came as a culture shock and as a learning experience that played a big role in his life. He became inspired to work as a teacher through his time at Gallaudet. Gunner has the passion to teach and make some differences in the world. He has worked with all grade levels, sharing his passion for learning with all students while providing them with the opportunity to find their place in the Deaf community and let their Deaf identity shine. Gunner is currently an ASL teacher at Plainfield South High School; he wants to teach students ASL and Deaf Culture.

"It is important to set your goals and vision that aligns with your passion. But it is even more important to get up and act passionately every single day toward it. Success is the reaction for every action you do on preparation, hard work, and learning from failure."

Dr. Andy Tao

American-Born Chinese, The Creative Builder, CEO and Producer of Blue20

Dr. Andy Tao, driven by a fervent enthusiasm for structured and imaginative endeavors, embarked on an academic journey culminating in a Ph.D. His insatiable curiosity and dedication manifested in a dissertation centered on unraveling health disparities within the deaf and hard of hearing populations, reflecting his commitment to accessibility and inclusivity.

Motivated by the profound impact of his research and 15 years of teaching, Andy channeled his passion into the entrepreneurial realm, birthing the innovative venture known as Blue20. At its core, Blue20 aspires to revolutionize the landscape of digital media, striving not only to enhance accessibility for the deaf community, but to extend the benefits of inclusivity to all.

www.theblue20.com

"Through my own hearing loss journey, I have realized that I am the only one that has lived my life and I need to embrace all of the ups and downs. Through a tapestry of life events, I have woven a life of purpose. My personal journey of living life with hearing loss has created a village of personal and professional connections that I would not have otherwise known.

Someone once told me that I could not be an audiologist due to my hearing loss. Even though this was crushing, it was the fuel that I needed to pour onto the fire to shine brighter! Don't let anyone limit you because of their belief. When there is a will, there is a way! Weave a bright tapestry of your own life because YOU are were created to bring your colors to brighten this world."

Carrie Spangler

Carrie Spangler

Audiologist and Coach

Carrie Spangler, Au.D, CCC-A, is a dedicated and respected professional in the field of educational audiology with over 25 years of experience. She also has a passionate personal journey with hearing loss. Dr. Spangler has turned what many view as a "disability" into an "ability." She also has a blog (hearingspanglish.blog) and podcast (empowEAR Audiology) which have international reach. Empowering and helping others with hearing differences, families, and professionals is at the core of her daily work. She has a proven track record developing, implementing, and sustaining programs including educational audiology programs. Dr. Spangler has numerous peer- and non-peer-reviewed publications and has presented topics related to educational audiology, advocacy, and peer support at the state, national, and international level. She obtained her coaching certification in 2024. In 2021, she was presented with the prestigious Fellow Award from the American Speech and Hearing Association.

www.empowearcoaching.com

> "To succeed, you have to believe in one Chinese quote – 'first bitter, sweet later.'
>
> To allow and show your passion, be you and believe in yourself because you are the only one that knows the best about yourself."

Clara Leung
Founder of Clara's Green House

I didn't set out to launch a side hustle selling plants on Facebook Marketplace — it kind of just happened, and I ended up founding a business called Clara's Green House which specializes in selling plants, teaching about plants and Old Chinese Feng Shui philosophy, and providing individuals and businesses Feng Shui consultations. Seriously, I grew up in Hong Kong, where I would watch my green-thumbed mother care for plants — some that she'd even clip right from nature and bring inside to nurture indoors — and learn about the art of Feng Shui. The joy plants brought my mother and the connection we forged because of plants has left a deep impression on me. Although Clara's Green House is my side business, I currently work as an accountant at one of the federal agencies in Washington, D.C. — I call it my passion project. Running Clara's Green House brings me joy and lets me help and coach people on Feng Shui their homes, utilizing Old Chinese Feng Shui practice properly.

www.clarasgreenhouse.com

NINA CUTRO-KELLY

WOMEN'S JUDO   GOLD

"Wake up every day grateful. Do what you love. Even on bad days, set goals and try to reach them. Don't let anything stop you."

Nina Cutro-Kelly
Judo Olympian and Deaflympic Champion

Nina Cutro-Kelly is a 2021 U.S. Judo Olympian, 2x SAMBO Super World Cup Champion, Deaflympic Champion, and 10x Senior National Judo Champion. Nina was the oldest American judoka ever to qualify for the Olympic Games. She is also a USA Judo Certified International Level Coach.

Nina has her Bachelor's in Political Science and French Language/Literature, and an MBA and a Master's in Applied Linguistics.

Nina is fluent in French and is a dual French/American citizen. @monkeyjudo (Instagram)

"If you have no experience, no matter how hard or terrible your career or job is, it is okay to start low and work your way up for experiences and eventually you'll get to where you wanna be. Know your worth!"

Luis Angel Fernandez
Diesel Mechanic

Hello! My name is Luis Fernandez. I'm 26 years old and I like video games and pitbulls. I've been working as a diesel mechanic for 4 1/2 years. I went to the Technology Center of DuPage and Kishwaukee College to learn automotive and diesel technology. It was a tough journey to get where I am now.

My first job was messy – oil everywhere, few equipment, and I got paid less than other mechanics. Once I had more experience fixing and learning how to communicate with other co-workers and drivers, and had more tools for the jobs I needed, I was able to get into high-paying jobs and achieved my dream.

"There's no one way to succeed, whether it's doing something or choosing a decision. Every person has their own way of doing life. Listen to others and yourself.

Stepping out of your comfort zone takes you to places larger than you could ever imagine!"

Karlie Waldrip
Author and Deaf Dog Advocate

Hi y'all! This is Karlie Waldrip; I am the author of "I Deaf-initely Can, Rhett the Heeler." I was born deaf and raised in Texas! I have a wide range of experience as a deaf person. I grew up wearing hearing aids, and then later decided to get cochlear implants as a tool to allow me to hear more sounds around me. I grew up learning how to talk and sign.

I taught as a Deaf Education teacher for 4 years! I adopted Rhett, who is a deaf dog from a small town shelter in Texas. I am currently a busy stay-at-home-mom and an author traveling all over sharing our story.

www.rhetttheheeler.com

"Have fun through all of life – with love, faith, and patience."

Carl and Susan Seabaugh
Owners of Cloves Woodworking

Life is full of surprises. Carl had a stroke and had to reconsider his profession. Carl rediscovered his passion for woodworking and helping others to enjoy top-quality wood pieces. Combining Carl's woodworking experience and his wife Susan's creativity, they created unique cutting boards and it was a huge hit. Overnight, Cloves Woodworking was formed.

www.cloveswoodworking.com

"Struggling is hard and painful. When you're thinking about quitting, remember your 'why.' It can feel overwhelming when looking at the big goal; it might feel impossible. However, focus on the small triumphs and take these triumphs to overcome your struggle one step at a time. Paso a paso. These small triumphs build confidence, and it keeps growing. You are the only thing that can move towards these steps."

Mia White
Soccer Pro

I was born and raised in Denver, Colorado, as the only deaf member in a hearing family. My parents and two brothers know American Sign Language (ASL) to communicate with me. I played 4 years of college soccer at the Rochester Institute of Technology and then went to Spain for a year to play soccer. After returning to the United States, I continued training to improve my skills and I am currently playing professionally in Finland. I am adapting to different cultures as the only Deaf player on their team and facing adversity in their journey. Additionally, I am on the US Deaf National Women's Soccer Team, and we won gold at the 2022 Deaflympics in Brazil and at the World Deaf Football Championships in Malaysia in 2023.

"Every challenge you encounter is a crucial step on your path to building resilience, self-worth, and confidence. Even when these experiences are difficult and painful, they shape who you are. Embracing your emotions is a vital part of being human and helps you gain deeper self-awareness. Develop a deep appreciation for your own company and learn to enjoy your own presence. Advocate for yourself, prioritize your mental health, and remember that living with adversity is an essential part of finding your strength and passion."

Rebecca Alexander

Rebecca Alexander

Psychotherapist, Author, Keynote Speaker, Disability Rights Advocate, Extreme Athlete, Unapologetic Badass

Rebecca Alexander is an award-winning author, psychotherapist, disability rights advocate, group fitness and yoga/meditation instructor, and extreme athlete who is almost completely blind and deaf. Rebecca is a Lululemon Athletica and fitness ambassador and has shared her journey on platforms like "The Today Show," NBC Nightly News, and CNN. Her inspiring story and mantra, "Breathe In Peace, Breathe Out Fear," were featured by GAPFit for International Women's Day. Swimming from Alcatraz to shore in the San Francisco Bay, summiting Mt. Kilimanjaro, participating in the 600-mile AIDS Lifecycle ride, and competing in Civilian Military Combine (CMC) races are a few of Rebecca's extraordinary feats. Rebecca is best known for her drive, zest for life, innate curiosity, remarkable sense of humor, and willingness to address difficult topics most people avoid. Consistently upbeat, Rebecca gives encouragement and inspiration to others who are facing their own challenges.

www.rebeccaalexander.org

Aistė Rye Manfredini

Visual Artist and Educator

Aistė Manfredini (she/her), also known by the artist name Aistė Rye, is a Lithuanian-American, Queer, Deaf/Hard of Hearing visual artist, muralist, and educator. Aistė is the founder of The Spirit Lab, an educational workshop series that brings therapeutic art to individuals and communities to experience the healing benefits of creative expression. She was born in Klaipėda and spent her childhood in Lithuania, immigrating to Chicago in 2000. She holds an M.A. in Emerging Media Design and Development and a B.A. in Journalism from Ball State University.

As a Deaf and Queer woman raised in post-Soviet Lithuania and coming of age in America, Aistė engages with the world from a position that transcends multiple cultural binaries. Aistė's artwork is informed by her experiences navigating an able-bodied and patriarchal society and seeks to challenge assumptions about culture, gender, feminism, and the Deaf experience.

Aistė's dreamlike paintings intend to take the audience on spiritual journeys into the surreal, inviting viewers to return to the ultimate path: the journey into ourselves. She most recently curated DEAFhood: Reflections on Identity and Deaf Culture at Slip Gallery in November 2022. Aistė's latest De'VIA-inspired murals can be found at the Northwest School for Deaf and Hard of Hearing Children and the 63rd St. Mural for Seattle's Phinney Neighborhood. www.aisteryecreative.com

"Living life with passion and success is a commitment to following my intuition and desires, trusting myself in challenging moments, being curious, and defining my version of success. When we listen to our intuition or the 'inner knowing' voice, we can see more clearly where to focus our energy to make a difference in our communities and the world. When we trust ourselves to follow our passions or desires, we are more likely to feel fulfilled, and as a result, successful. This can be challenging to do when there are expectations, norms, and pressures from inner circles and society at large who have ideas of what success looks like. However, a commitment to listening to your intuition and following your unique path over and over again, despite how difficult, is one of the most important skills to learn in life. For me, this approach builds self-confidence and integrity, and ultimately, leads me to my version of success and happiness."

Aistė Rye Manfredini

"Dreams and ideas of what you're passionate about or what you consider to be success will change over time. I often see people refusing to 'let go' because it may represent failure on their part. The reality, as the Australian comedian Tim Minchin once said, is that in pursuing the big shiny dreams that we're no longer excited about, we often miss the better opportunities in our peripheral vision.

Rather – celebrate the small victories that you achieve every year, month, week, and day. Cumulatively, those victories are far more meaningful to you, those you love, and those that love you."

Neil McDevitt

Neil McDevitt

**Mayor,
North Wales Borough**

Neil McDevitt is the Mayor for North Wales Borough in Suburban Philadelphia. He is the first Deaf person to be directly elected to this office in the country. Neil is also the Treasurer of the North Wales Water Authority.

Neil is the Executive Director for the Deaf-Hearing Communication Centre in Swarthmore, PA. Previously, Neil served at the Federal Emergency Management Agency in their Office of Disability Integration and Coordination.

As a former volunteer firefighter in suburban Philadelphia, Neil was one of a handful of emergency responders in the country who are also profoundly deaf.

He graduated from Gallaudet University in 1996 with a degree in Government. He lives in the Borough with his wife, two children, a lizard, and two dogs.

"Life is all about perspective."

Ronnie Cuartero

Chef Ronnie

Born and raised in Daly City, CA (San Francisco area), I attended the Rochester Institute of Technology/National Institute for the Deaf (RIT/NTID).

During my journey, I participated in several amazing events, including crossing America by bicycle, a Lego contest, and a Favorite Chef contest.

Currently, I reside in Rochester and work as a chef at Golden Harvest Bakery and Café, where cooking has become my passion that I want to share with the world through my culinary arts.

"When you feel a path has become blocked, harness your courage and creativity to carve out a new path for yourself."

Haben Girma

Author, Keynote Speaker, and Attorney

Photo by Darius Bashar

The first Deafblind person to graduate from Harvard Law School, Haben Girma is a human rights lawyer advancing disability justice. President Obama named her a White House Champion of Change, and the World Health Organization appointed her Commissioner of Social Connection. She received the Helen Keller Achievement Award, a spot on the Forbes 30 Under 30 list, and TIME100 Talks.

Haben believes disability is an opportunity for innovation, and she travels the world teaching organizations the importance of choosing inclusion. She is also the bestselling author of Haben: The Deafblind Woman Who Conquered Harvard Law.

www.habengirma.com

What does success mean to you?

YOU are a beautiful gift to the world.

Made in the USA
Las Vegas, NV
23 September 2024

95697336R00095